Revise for Geography GCSE OCR/WJEC Specification B
(Avery Hill)

Second Edition

Stuart Currie

Heinemann Educational Publishers
Halley Court, Jordan Hill, Oxford, OX2 8EJ
Part of Harcourt Education Ltd.
Heinemann is the registered trademark of Harcourt Education Ltd.

Text © Stuart Currie
First published in 2000
Second Edition 2002
07 06 05 04
10 9 8 7 6 5 4 3

British Library Cataloguing in Publication Data

A catalogue record for this book is available from the British Library

ISBN 0 435 09973 6
Original illustrations © Harcourt Education Limited 2000
Illustrated by Jane Bottomley and Joe Little

Designed and typeset by AMR Ltd
Printed in the UK by Bath Press Ltd

Acknowledgements

The author and publishers would like to thank the following for the use of copyright material:

Photographs: Collections (p.64, 4.5); Cumbrian Library/Geoff Berry (p.57, 3.18); Emscher Park, Germany (p.94, P); Format/Maggie Murray (p.47, 3.7); Lucky Goldstar (p.92, L); National Geographic Society/Ben Curtis (p.87, E); Panos Pictures/David Reed (p.36, 2.14); Popperfoto/Reuters (p.87, C, D); Rex Features (p.94, O); Richmond and Rigg (p.93, M); Robert Harding Picture Library (p.87, A); Roger Scruton (p.90, H); Skyscan (p.89, G); Still Pictures/C. Martin (p.87, B); Still Pictures/N. Dickinson (p.26, 1.24); Stuart Currie (p.36, 2.15); UNDP (p.93, N); University of Dundee (p.18, 1.10);

Maps and diagrams: Human Development Report (p.62, 4.2, 4.3); Leicester City Council (p.91, map J); The Meteorological Office (p.18, 1.9, 1.10); *New Internationalist*/Jeremy Seabrook (p.47, 3.6; p.48, 3.8); Maps/mapping data licensed from Ordnance Survey® with the permission of The Controller of Her Majesty's Stationery Office © Crown copyright. All rights reserved. Licence no.100000230 (p.59, 3.21; p.88, map F; p.92, K); © *Times* Newspapers Ltd, London, 5/7/96 (p.35, 2.12); Welsh Development Agency (p.67, 4.12); *The Independent on Sunday* (p.73, 4.17).

The publishers have made every effort to contact the copyright holders of material published in this book. Any omissions will be rectified in subsequent printings if notice is given to the publishers.

Contents

Introduction

This book has been written to help you get the best possible result in your GCSE geography examinations. There are a number of different geography Specifications. This book is aimed only at students entered for Avery Hill Geography: OCR/WJEC Specification B.

It is therefore ideal for students following the Avery Hill Specification because it targets you directly.

As you will see from the early pages of this book, there is a great deal to know about getting the best out of a geography examination that has little to do with the actual geography. Don't ignore these opening pages, though, because they are one of the keys to your examination success. There are many candidates who enter the examination each year who are very good geographers but never quite have the ability to show it in the examination.

How to use this book

First a word of caution. This revision guide is not intended to replace your teacher. Most of you will have followed a two-year course of study in preparation for your GCSE examinations. You will have notes in either a file or an exercise book that are a record of your course of study and the *real* key to your success in the examinations. This revision guide will, therefore, help you make sense of your notes and train you how to use them to get the best possible result in the written examinations. Your teacher will also be working hard for your examination success and it is intended that the revision guide helps in this process.

Use of special features

This revision guide contains special features designed to help you work painlessly through your revision schedule – or at least as painlessly as possible!

Hints and Tips! When you see this symbol you will find points of general advice about how to prepare for the examination and also how to approach the examination itself.

Action Point

Things to do, including activities to focus your revision and test yourself. If you do well, be pleased with yourself. If at first you don't do well, re-read the section and test yourself again.

Know your Case Study

In each unit of this revision guide you will be taken through the main geographical principles you need for the examination. Many of these are demonstrated through Case Studies. You may wish to use these in the Case Study sections of Papers 1 and 2. You have also developed your own Case Studies as you worked through the geography course. Use matrices to organise these, and through the questions in each unit, practise selecting information from them to answer the questions set.

Use the tables on pages 75–80 to match your own Case Studies to questions that have appeared in recent examinations.

 This symbol occurs with important information about the examination.

The Avery Hill Geography Specification

The Avery Hill Specification consists of four units:
Unit 1: Climate, the environment and people
- What is weather?
  - how are people affected by weather?
- What is climate?
  - how do people affect climate?
  - how are people affected by climate?
  - how can people change weather and climate?
- How do ecosystems operate?
  - how do people affect ecosystems?
  - how are people affected by ecosystems?
  - how might ecosystems be managed in a sustainable way?

Unit 2: Water, landforms and people
- How does the hydrological cycle operate?
- How is a sustainable supply of fresh water provided?
- What are drought and flooding?
  – how do these affect people?
- How does water shape river valleys and coasts?
- How do river and coastal landforms and their processes affect people?
- How are river and coastal landforms and their processes affected by people?

Unit 3: People and place
- What influences standard of living and quality of life?
- What affects access to housing and services?
- How are towns and cities changing?
  – how might towns and cities be planned for sustainability?
- Why does migration take place between countryside and cities?
- What are the effects of migrations on the areas people leave and those they move to?
- How does short-term movement of people from towns and cities affect countryside areas?

Unit 4: People, work and development
- How and why do employment opportunities differ from place to place and with time?
- How are economic and social well-being measured?
- What is meant by development and economic development?
- How and why are countries at different stages of development identified?
- How does international trade/aid take place and how does it affect people and countries?
- What factors influence industrial location?
- How do large companies influence employment and economic development?

- How might economic activity seriously damage the environment?
- How may conflict between job creation and environmental damage be sustainably managed?

⚠ Action Point

These are the main questions that you have been exploring through your GCSE geography course. Your notes will include a number of Case Studies designed to answer most of these questions. Do a matching exercise to show yourself where your notes are targeting these questions. You may wish to make a larger copy of the matrix below and create your own for the other three units.

Hints and Tips!

Filling in the matrix

Case Study: write the name of the Case Study in this column. Name the country in which it is located. State whether it is an LEDC or MEDC. This might help you make decisions when selecting the correct Case Study to use in the examination.

Page number: if your notes are numbered, this will give you easy reference at a later stage in your revision. If you can find the correct notes quickly, there will be little lost time and your precious revision time will be used effectively.

Main points: reduce your Case Study to just a small number of simple statements – use bullet points. When you get into the examination room these statements will help you recall the greater detail you have in your notes.

Questions	Case Study	Page number	Main points
What is weather?			
How are people affected by weather?			
What is climate?			
How are people affected by climate?			
How can people affect weather and climate?			
How do ecosystems operate?			
How do people affect ecosystems?			
How are people affected by ecosystems?			
How might ecosystems be managed in a sustainable way?			

▲ *Matrix for Climate, the environment and people*

Assessment through the Avery Hill Specification

The terminal examination consists of two papers. These are totally different from each other. You will be entered for either the Foundation Tier or the Higher Tier, so you will do either Papers 1 and 3 or Papers 2 and 4.

Paper 1 (Foundation Tier) and Paper 2 (Higher Tier)

These papers consist of six questions with two on each of three of the units in the Specification. Answer one question on each unit.

Paper 3 (Foundation Tier) and Paper 4 (Higher Tier)

This examines the fourth Specification unit and is a problem-solving exercise. You will be asked to use information to help you present plans and justify your ideas.

Different years – different units!

The units of the Specification that are tested by the two sets of examination papers change each year. You will find below the ways in which your examination will sample the four units.

Papers 1 and 2	Papers 3 and 4
Climate, the environment and people	People and place
Water, landforms and people	
People, work and development	

◀ 2003

Papers 1 and 2	Papers 3 and 4
Climate, the environment and people	Water, landforms and people
People and place	
People, work and development	

◀ 2004

The level of entry

By the Foundation Tier route. This opens up Grades C to G.

Component	% of marks	Length
Paper 1 Consists of 3 sections Answer 1 question from each section.	45%	1 hr 30 mins
Paper 3 A problem-solving paper Answer all questions.	30%	1 hr 30 mins
Coursework A Study and a Cross-Unit Task	25%	completed before the examination

By the Higher Tier route. This opens up Grades A* to D.

Component	% of marks	Length
Paper 2 Consists of 3 sections Answer 1 question from each section.	45%	1 hr 30 mins
Paper 4 A problem-solving paper Answer all questions.	30%	1 hr 30 mins
Coursework A Study and a Cross-Unit Task	25%	completed before the examination

The decision to enter the examinations through the Foundation Tier or Higher Tier is often an easy one. For some people, though, it is very difficult. It partly depends on your expectations and the needs you have from your final result. If, for example, you wish to study geography at Advanced or AS Level, you will probably need to enter through the Higher Tier to get the grade required for further studies in the subject. It also depends on how you cope with examinations and how well you did with your coursework.

There are differences in the way the examination papers are presented:
- Foundation Tier papers are more structured; Higher Tier papers are less so.
- Foundation Tier papers demand relatively short responses; Higher Tier papers demand longer answers.
- Foundation Tier Paper 1 is answered in a question/answer booklet that indicates the length of the answer by the number of lines provided for your response. Higher Tier Paper 2 is answered on lined paper. You will need to organise the length of your responses.

Examination entry by the Foundation Tier Route is *not* a sign of failure – it is merely a realistic decision being made to help you gain the best possible grade.

Effective revision

How do you revise effectively? There is no simple answer to this question, merely hints on how to get the best out of your available time. Some people need total silence in order to perform well; others need to listen to a CD. Some people are able to concentrate for hours; others have a much shorter concentration span and, therefore, will need to structure their revision into much smaller

parcels of time. The only effective way for you to revise is the one that suits you best. A word of warning, though – don't adopt a strategy that is pleasant for you but *doesn't* help the revision process. Listening to music can be fun and helps many in their revision. If it doesn't help you concentrate, though, it will set you back a great deal and probably result in a lower grade. You must be honest with yourself. There is a long period of time between the examinations and your results. You will only enjoy that time fully if you have been completely honest with yourself during the revision process. Although there are no set strategies that will work for all people, there are a number of ideas that will help you succeed:
- Don't leave your revision to the last minute. Read your notes as you work through the course. Revision is what it says it is: looking back through notes on ideas that you already understand and have stored away somewhere in the back of your memory.
- As you work through the course, don't be afraid to ask your teacher for additional explanation of any areas of work you don't understand. Work that is fully understood when you tackle it the first time will help you more than trying to come to terms with it at the last minute. And don't forget, when you ask for an explanation of a process or idea in the classroom, there will be other grateful people in the group who did not have the courage to ask for themselves.
- When you are given study leave by your school or college, make sure that you attend all the advertised geography lessons that are being offered. These will help you to prepare fully for the examinations.

- Work out a realistic revision timetable that takes into account the demands of all your other subjects and the time you have available during a typical school week and holiday week. It should also take into account your own individual concentration span and the timing of your examinations. Use the table on p.14 to help you organise your time.
- Find a space where you are happy to revise and you can concentrate. You must feel comfortable during the revision process. You may, for example, need to ask people at home to turn down the volume of a television, radio or stereo.
- There *is* a happy balance that can be achieved between revision and the other demands being made on your time. Your social life need not disappear altogether!
- Reward yourself. If there is something you wish to watch on television, plan an hour's revision before it. Watch the programme as a reward for reaching your targets.
- And finally, if you feel you are not coping, then ask for help. Don't let things get on top of you. The earlier you ask, the more people will be able to help you. Remember that your teachers and family want you to succeed.

Action Point

Make sure your notes are tidy!
It also helps to number sheets in a file, so if the file mysteriously opens and deposits its contents on the floor, it's not a huge disaster.

Revision strategies

For almost all people, *passive revision* does not work effectively. Merely staring at a page of your notes is only likely to work for a very short period of time. It is not long before your attention will be drawn to other attractions that have nothing to do with your work – examining posters on your wall, for example.

Active revision, on the other hand, involves you in *doing* something. This very act will help keep your concentration at a high level and should result in a product that will help the later stages of the revision process.

You might attempt to:
- make revision cards. These are especially effective for revising Case Studies.

- use spider diagrams or webs. These are helpful when linking several influences on one feature, like reasons for the decline of an industry or the way in which the multiplier effect works.
- test yourself on the main terms used in each unit of the Specification. Write the terms on separate cards. Do the same for the meanings. Jumble them up and then try to match them together again.
- practise drawing sketches and sketch maps that can be used in the examination room. Try to memorise one and then put it away. Attempt to sketch it, then compare your results with the original.

Examples of these strategies are shown later in this revision guide.

Tackling examination questions

You may not believe it, but the examination is set up to help you. It is not intended to trick you or to find out what you don't know. Its purpose is to find out what you know, understand and can do:
- *to know* – it tests your knowledge of important geographical terms and the Case Studies you have learned.
- *to understand* – it tests how well you can *apply* geographical principles and processes you have learned in the classroom to new situations. It also tests your understanding of how to use the information you have learned in your Case Studies to answer the questions set by the examiner and not just to write all you know about a place or an issue.
- *to do* – it tests your ability to read and complete maps, graphs, diagrams and other resources that are found in the paper.

The first thing to remember when looking at an examination paper is that *all* the information given to you by the examiner is for your use. It is important that you:
- read the instructions on the cover of the paper. They contain information that will help you get full value out of the paper. You should be able to see copies in school. The front of a paper doesn't change much, if at all, from year to year. Make sure you are familiar with the instructions well in advance of the examination.
- do exactly as instructed by the examiner. The first paper you will sit asks you to answer *one* question from each of *three* sections on the paper. Do *exactly* that, so that you answer a

total of three questions in the examination. Doing anything else is likely to result in you getting a grade that is poorer than you otherwise deserve.

● know how to react to each of the *command terms* you come across. Command terms are a number of words that the examiner uses to tell you what to do when answering particular questions or parts of questions. Many of them are used in all your examination subjects; others are peculiar to only one or two of them.

Common command terms

The command terms most commonly used in the geography examination include:

Circle   You will be asked to circle the correct answer from a number of options listed on the paper.

Compare   You are being asked to say what is similar and different between two pieces of information. The use of a word like 'whereas' will help you to make the comparison.

Complete   This could be asked in a number of ways:
'Complete the graph or map using these figures.'
'Complete the sentence below.'

Describe   This is something that causes difficulty for many students. You are only being asked to say what is there. It could be the scene in a photo or a pattern on a map, a distribution, a location. It is not asking you to say *why* it is there: that is *explaining*.

Draw   This could be the instruction to draw a sketch map to show the location or distribution of features when answering a Case Study question. It could also be asking you to draw your plans, sometimes on a map provided, in Section C of the problem-solving paper.

Explain/give reasons for
These terms are asking you to say why something that you have already described exists or has happened. It will often be written as 'give two reasons to explain'. Make sure that you give the number of reasons requested.

You are often asked to give 'two reasons' that are worth 4 marks. In this case there are 2 marks for each reason and you must give an elaborated response. That is a simple statement and its elaboration. The elaboration is sometimes called a 'So what?' response. There will be practice of this at several points later in this book.

Justify   You are being asked to explain why you have made a decision. *Justify* is a term you are most likely to come across in Part C of the problem-solving paper. If you break it down, you are not only being asked to explain why your choice is a good one but also to say why you did not choose other options that were open to you. Every question is different but it might be possible to work to a structure that is suitable for many *justify* questions:

● I have decided to ...
● The main advantages of my scheme are ...
● It does have the following disadvantages ... but it is the best scheme for the needs of the area.
● It will benefit the environment/ people (who or whatever you have been asked to consider) because ...
● I considered other ideas including ... Although they had some good points, the following disadvantages led me to reject them ...

List Simply that. Make a list of features you see on a map, photograph or other resource on the paper. The danger, especially on the Higher Tier, is to write too much. It is only a list!

Locate Say where a place is. You are usually asked to locate a Case Study. If possible, name the area and country your Case Study is from. Make sure that the location you choose helps answer the question that has been asked. If it asks for an LEDC, don't use an MEDC example. You may wish to draw a sketch map to show location.

Measure A command term that asks you to take *accurate* measurements from a resource like an OS map. Don't just guess – measure it accurately. The examiner will allow some leeway in your answer – but not much!

Name This is asking you to give only the name or names of some feature(s) from a map or other resource. Use the resource carefully and don't be tempted, especially on the Higher Tier Paper 2, to write too much.

Read An instruction simply to read the information that is there. Just because there is no response expected from you, doesn't mean that you need not do it. You will not be able to answer the questions that come after if you do not follow the instructions carefully.

Study/ look at A similar instruction to the previous term. Study the resource carefully and use detail from it in your responses.

Suggest You will probably be asked to *suggest* why a feature you have described is as it is. This term is similar to *explain* but tells you that you are expected to bring in ideas and understanding of your own that are not provided on the paper.

Use (evidence)

This command term will be used when directing you to a resource: a map, graph, table, news extract, photograph. It is asking you to quote directly from that resource. You will not gain full marks for the question unless you do so. For example, a question that asks you to use evidence from an OS map will expect you to quote such information as grid references and names of the features you are describing.

What is meant by

This is asking you to give a definition of a geographical term that you should know. Geography has its own technical language that you have been learning throughout your school life. You will be expected to know this for the examination. Many of the definitions you will be expected to know are found later in this revision guide.

Other terms

The command terms above expect you to respond in a particular way. There are other terms we use in geography that could also appear in your examination. They are not specifically about any of the four units you have studied but could appear anywhere in either of the papers you sit.

Accessibility

This is asking you to use the location of a place for a purpose. How easy is it for people to get to? Answers to such questions could be written as: 'It is inaccessible/accessible to ... because ...'.

Distribution

You are being asked to describe how something is spread out. It could be distribution of features on a map or on a graph. In which places are there more? In which places are there less? On maps, use features like the city centre or compass directions to help your description. On graphs, use information on the bottom axis, for example the months and seasons on a climate graph.

If you are asked for a description of distribution, do *not* explain why the feature is spread out the way it is. That will probably be the next question.

Location   Where a place is. Usually you will be asked to describe a location using a map provided on the paper. Locations are often well described by quoting the direction and distance from another point on the map. If you are asked for a description of a location, do *not* explain why it is there. That, again, will probably be the next question.

Patterns   If you are being asked to describe a pattern it could be a *distribution* or a trend that is expected. This will depend on the resource you are using.

Sustainable   This term is used to indicate that something is being managed in such a way as to be capable of being of benefit to future generations.

Trend   Usually used when asking you about what a graph shows. General statements like *rise and fall* are useful. Describing the rate at which this is happening will also help you gain marks. It is also useful to quote evidence from the resource (see *Use evidence*).

Other points to consider

Case Studies

On Papers 1 and 2 you will face the Case Study. The Case Study section comes at the end of each question. Many students find it useful to read the Case Studies in each pair of questions carefully before deciding which question to answer. The first parts of each question test your ability to use resources and demonstrate your understanding of the geography they show. If you answer these and then reach a Case Study you cannot answer, you will waste a large number of marks. So read the Case Study to help you decide which is the best question to answer.

Make sure that you are clear as to what the examiner is asking. Write about only that.

This does not mean that you should answer the Case Study first. All the questions on your examination paper have been written to help you most if you start at the beginning of each question and work your way towards the end.

How much should I write?

This is an important question because if you write too much, you may run out of time and not reach the end of the paper. If you write too little, you may not put down enough ideas or detail to be given full marks for the question.

There are two ways the examiner tells you how much you are expected to write:

1   At the end of each part of a question there is a number in brackets. For example:

    Describe the location of ...   [2]

    This is telling you that there are 2 marks available for this question and that you should give two pieces of information in order to obtain those marks. Using a question asking for the location of a place on a map, you could write 'It is so many kilometres (1 mark) in such a direction (1 mark) from another named place on the map.' You have now said enough and any extra effort would be wasting your ink and valuable time.

2 Both Foundation Tier papers are printed in question/answer booklets. The examiner has left enough space after each part-question for a person with average-sized writing to fill. Of course, if your handwriting is very small, you will probably not need all the space, but if it is huge, you may have to finish your answer on the extra pages found at the back of the booklet. If you need to do this, it is *important* that you carefully write the number of the question you are continuing to answer. Your examiner is not a mind reader!

Those of you who are entered for the Higher Tier will need to be even more careful than those on the Foundation Tier. Although your problem-solving paper (Paper 4) is in a question/answer booklet, you will have to answer your first paper (Paper 2) in a booklet that consists of only lined paper. This means that *your* only guide in this paper will be the bracketed marks. Be careful. There is a tendency with most people, especially when they are confident, to write too much.

Levels of response marks

Most of the marks you will gain on both your examination papers will be the result of what the examiners call *points* marking. On this type of question you will gain a mark for each valid point you make. In the example on the preview page you gained one mark for stating the distance and another for the direction of a place from another point. You made two separate, but related, points.

Levels of response marking is different and is mainly found in the Case Study sections on Papers 1 and 2 and in Section C of Papers 3 and 4. This type of marking looks more at the *quality* of your answer. You may write a huge amount, all of which is accurate, but never rise above a very low level. If you provide much description and don't show a great deal of understanding, it is likely that your marks will be low.

The levels of response mark scheme below, that could be used with the Sanjay Gandhi Nagar problem-solving exercise on page 48, may explain why.

Level 1	An almost purely descriptive response with little detail on the plan and only simple reasons to justify the choice that could apply to any squatter settlement. Information is communicated by brief statements.	**1–3 marks**
Level 2	Through the plan and report, different land uses are developed with detailed justification to specifically meet the needs of people in Sanjay Gandhi Nagar. Communication may be wordy or illogical. A limited number of geographical terms are used. There is some accuracy in spelling, punctuation and grammar.	**4–6 marks**
Level 3	This is an integrated plan that caters for the needs of the people of Sanjay Gandhi Nagar. The choice of strategies is justified with sophisticated reasoning. It is written as a letter and a range of geographical terms is used. Spelling, punctuation and grammar have considerable accuracy.	**7 marks**

Perhaps you can see how the ideas become more complex as the levels rise. It is not possible to gain the full 10 marks by merely giving seven simple reasons. That would not get you out of the first level!

❗Action Point

The jumps that are needed to get a piece of work from one level to another are known as *hurdles*. If you know what the hurdles are you are half-way towards being able to jump them. This can be shown by the progression of 'justification' from *simple* to *detailed* to *sophisticated* as you rise through the levels. Make a list of the other hurdles in the mark scheme on page 12 and in either of those below. They are from the Case Study questions on Paper 1 (Foundation Tier) and Paper 2 (Higher Tier).

Are you equipped for the examinations?

Finally, don't forget to take all the writing equipment you need into the examination room. You don't want anything to upset your concentration at this time.

If you have taken these pages seriously and practised the different strategies, your examination technique should be reaching a quite brilliant standard. This is of little use to you, though, if you do not fully understand the geographical content, ideas and skills.

That comes next ...

Paper 1 (Foundation)

Level 1	Gives simple description or explanation. Case Study may be inappropriate but is applied reasonably well. Information is communicated by brief statements.	**1–2 marks**
Level 2	Gives descriptive points with some explanation. Appropriate choice of Case Study applied well. Communication may be rambling or illogical. A limited number of specialist terms used. There is some accuracy in spelling, punctuation and grammar.	**3–4 marks**
Level 3	Provides a balanced account which includes specific description and explanation. Appropriate choice of Case Study applied very well. The written style has a suitable structure. There is a range of specialist terms. Spelling, punctuation and grammar have considerable accuracy.	**5 marks**

Paper 2 (Higher)

Level 1	Provides simple description or explanation only. Information is communicated by brief statements.	**1–2 marks**
Level 2	Provides account in which description is accompanied by some explanation. Choice of Case Study is applied reasonably well. Communication may be rambling or illogical. Limited use of specialist terms. Greater accuracy in spelling, punctuation and grammar.	**3–4 marks**
Level 3	Names an appropriate example. Provides a balanced account with accurate descriptive points and detailed explanation. Appropriate choice of Case Study applied well. Communication logical and clear. A range of specialist terms used. Some accuracy in spelling, punctuation and grammar.	**5–6 marks**
Level 4	Names an appropriate example. Provides a balanced account which includes specific detailed description and specific detailed explanation. Appropriate choice of Case Study applied very well. The written style has a suitable structure. There is a wide range of specialist terms. Spelling, punctuation and grammar have considerable accuracy.	**7–8 marks**

Table 1 – Revision timetable

	Week 1 & 7	Week 2 & 8	Week 3 & 9	Week 4 & 10	Week 5 & 11	Week 6 & 12
Monday						
Tuesday						
Wednesday						
Thursday						
Friday						
Saturday						
Sunday						

Unit 1: Climate, the environment and people

What are weather and climate?

Much of this unit relies on knowing the difference between weather and climate. *Weather* is the day-to-day changes in the atmosphere, whereas *climate* is the average of these changes over a time span of at least thirty years. The climate is, therefore, a statement of the conditions of such features as rainfall, temperature and sunshine that we can *expect* in a particular place during a particular month or season, and weather is what actually happens on a day-to-day basis.

◀ *1.1*   Weather conditions

◀ *1.2*   Climate data

What are weather systems?

Weather systems are air conditions that bring particular characteristic features of air pressure, precipitation, temperature and cloud cover to the areas they pass over. The United Kingdom experiences two major weather systems: depressions and anticyclones.

Depressions
- These are centres of low air pressure where warm air from the tropics and cool air from the polar regions meet.
- The dividing zones between the warm and cool air are known as *fronts*.
- In the northern hemisphere air spirals inwards to centres of depressions in an anticlockwise direction.
- Warm air rises over cold air and cools. The air is unstable, clouds form and precipitation occurs.

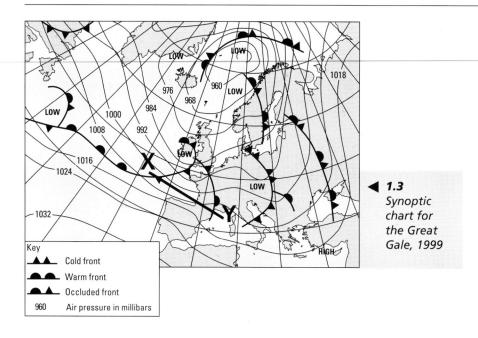

◀ **1.3** Synoptic chart for the Great Gale, 1999

Key

▲▲ Cold front

●● Warm front

●▲ Occluded front

960 Air pressure in millibars

Action Point

Using map 1.3, identify the warm front that is affecting France.

Using diagram 1.5, describe the movement of air at the warm front and the cold front. Explain how this movement causes (a) clouds, (b) precipitation.

Around 270 million trees were destroyed in France. This was 3% of the country's total woodland cover.

At least 33 people died in France, with a further 67 dying across Europe.

Road and bridge repairs cost the French government £165 m. Repairs to schools costs a further £100 m.

At Disneyland Paris, the theme park was closed and hotels evacuated.

◀ **1.4** Effects of the Great Storm

Hints and Tips!

Remember the difference between *describe* and *explain*.

Action Point

Use evidence from the synoptic chart (weather map) 1.3 to describe where the winds in the Great Gale were strongest. Using figure 1.4, list two different types of damage caused by the Great Gale. Explain two ways in which people could have protected property against the damage. Explain how accurate weather forecasting could reduce damage and loss of life.

The Great Gale that hit France and much of central Europe in December 1999 is an example of a severe depression. The air pressure at its centre was lower than is usually the case. It caused a great deal of damage because of the high winds and heavy rainfall it brought.

- Lines joining together points of equal atmospheric pressure on a synoptic chart (weather map) are called *isobars*.
- On a synoptic chart, the closer together the isobars, the faster the wind.

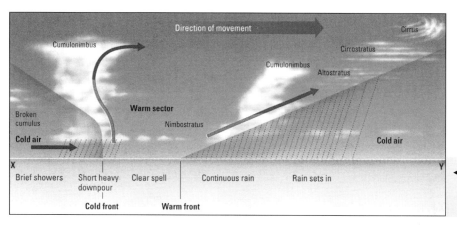

◀ **1.5** A cross-section through a depression (X–Y on map 1.3)

Severe tropical depressions in the Atlantic Ocean are known as *hurricanes*. In Asia they are called *cyclones* and *typhoons*. These storms only exist where in one area of the sea temperatures become greater than 27°C. The water vapour spirals up the centre of the hurricane and the energy that is given off as it cools powers the hurricane.

When hurricanes reach land they lose their power source and die out.

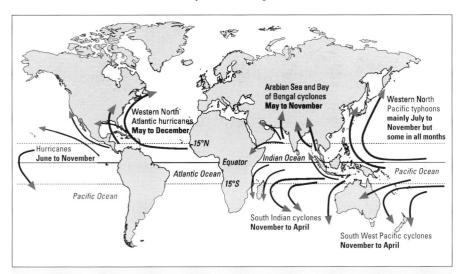

▲ *1.6 The distribution of severe tropical storms*

Action Point

Use map 1.6 to describe the distribution of severe tropical storms. Give two reasons to explain this distribution.

Hints and Tips!

It is likely that a question like 'Give two reasons to explain...' will be worth 4 marks. If it is, don't forget to give a 'So what?' answer.

23 Sept:
Starting in the Atlantic Ocean, Georges hits Dominica with 190 km/h winds. Sugar, banana and rice crops are wiped out.

25 Sept:
Over half a million people are evacuated in Florida.

27 Sept:
Georges cuts across S. Florida, ripping roofs off motels, uprooting palm trees and destroying electricity and telephone lines.

29 Sept:
After passing near New Orleans, Georges slows down over the land area of S. Mississippi.

▲ *1.7 Diary of a hurricane: Georges, 1998*

Know your Case Study

For a weather event you have studied, name its location, describe its effects and explain how people protected themselves and their property.

Action Point

Use the diary 1.7 to follow the route taken by Hurricane Georges. Describe the damage it caused. Suggest how the effects of Georges may have been different in Dominica (LEDC) and the USA (MEDC).

Anticyclones

Anticyclones are areas of high air pressure. Air spirals outwards in a clockwise direction in the northern hemisphere. Although the air pressures are similar in summer and winter, the weather brought by summer and winter anticyclones is totally different. This depends on a number of principles. In anticyclones:

- air in the centre is still or slow moving
- air is sinking and is therefore warming; this makes it stable with clear skies and no precipitation.

Summer anticyclones bring dry and hot weather that can stay for several days at a time. There is a large diurnal (daily) range of temperatures.

Action Point

A *summer anticyclone.* Describe the location of the centre of high pressure affecting the UK on map 1.9. Use evidence from map 1.9 to explain the cloud pattern shown in photo 1.10.

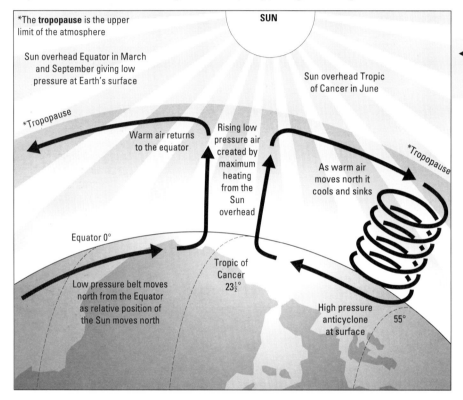

◀ **1.8** *The formation of summer anticyclones*

Hints and Tips!

Use the key on map 1.3, page 16 if you need one for chart 1.9.

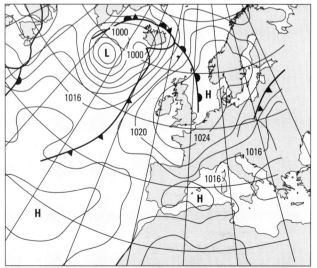

▲ **1.9** *Synoptic chart for 8 July 1999*

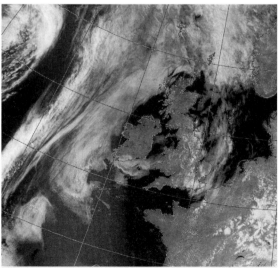

▲ **1.10** *Satellite image for 8 July 1999*

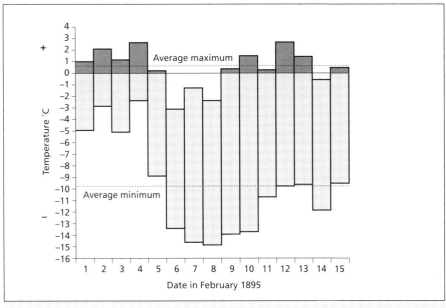

▲ **1.11** Diurnal (daily) maximum and minimum temperatures in Cambridge in February 1895

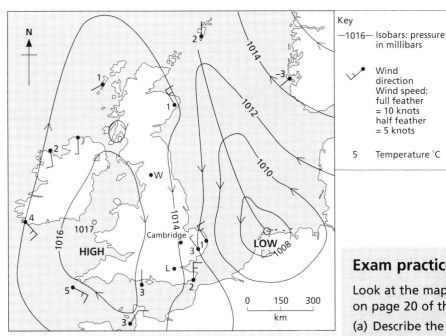

▲ **1.12** Synoptic chart of the weather conditions on 12 February 1895

Hints and Tips!

When a question asks you to *suggest* something, it is often asking you to explain what *you* think might happen.

Action Point

A *winter anticyclone*. Look at graph 1.11. What is the diurnal range of temperature on 8 February 1895? Give one reason for this range of temperature.

Describe the location of the centre of high air pressure on map 1.12. Describe the movement of air in the anticyclone.

Action Point

Explain how winter and summer anticyclones have different effects on people's activities.

Exam practice

Look at the maps and climate table 1.14 on page 20 of this revision guide.

(a) Describe the movement of wind in June. (1 mark)

(b) Compare the wind movement in July with that in December. (2 marks)

(c) Explain how the wind movement affects precipitation. (4 marks)

(d) Use photographs A and B in the colour resources section to suggest how the lives of people are affected by the monsoon climate. (4 marks)

How are people affected by climate?

Climate is controlled by a number of factors:

1.13

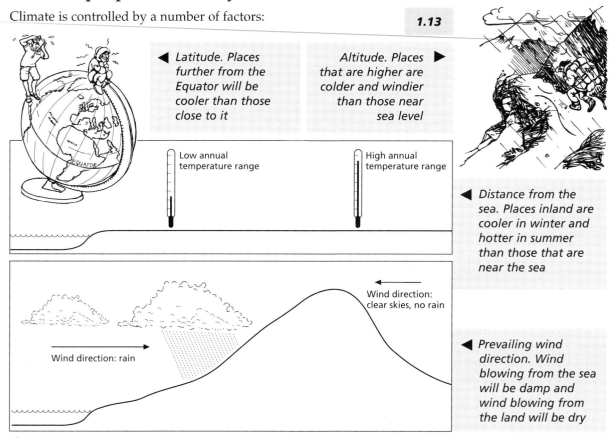

◀ *Latitude. Places further from the Equator will be cooler than those close to it*

Altitude. Places that are higher are colder and windier than those near sea level ▶

Low annual temperature range

High annual temperature range

◀ *Distance from the sea. Places inland are cooler in winter and hotter in summer than those that are near the sea*

Wind direction: clear skies, no rain

Wind direction: rain

◀ *Prevailing wind direction. Wind blowing from the sea will be damp and wind blowing from the land will be dry*

The regular patterns of air conditions shown by climate give an indication as to how people will run their daily lives. The seasonal changes in temperature and rainfall will dictate their lifestyle to a great extent.

The monsoon climate

	J	F	M	A	M	J	J	A	S	O	N	D
Temperature (°C)	24	24	25	28	29	28	27	26	26	27	26	24
Precipitation (mm)	3	0	3	0	18	523	694	409	300	61	10	0
Total precipitation = 2021 mm												

◀ **1.14** *Wet monsoon winds blow into India in June and dry monsoon winds blow out towards Australia in December*

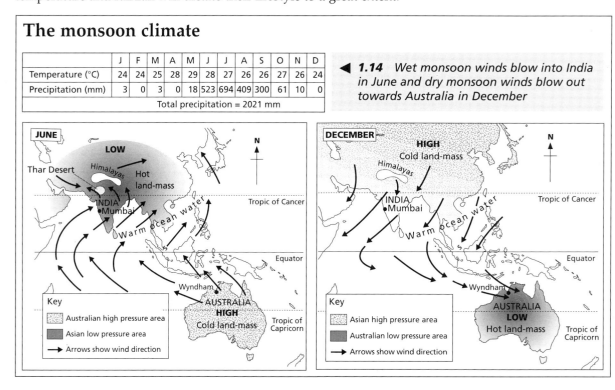

❗ Action Point

Use photos A and B in the colour resources section to describe the effects of the monsoon rain on people in India in June and July. Suggest two ways in which the lives of people will be different in December.

Know your Case Study

For a named climate you have studied, name the area affected by the climate, describe the climate, and explain how the climate affects the lives of people.

Exam Watch

The map and climate table 1.14 on page 20 are there to help you answer the Exam Practice question on page 19. Attempt that question now.

How do people affect climate?

Usually the ways in which people bring about climate change are unintentional. In some cases the changes that take place do not create problems for either the wider environment or the local area of the changes.

The creation of *urban heat islands*, for example, has resulted from the large amounts of heat given off by buildings and vehicles in large towns and cities. This makes urban centres much warmer than the surrounding countryside. In itself this does not create problems and few people worry a great deal that there is no longer ice-skating on the rivers of our major cities.

Global warming is far more worrying. Many experts believe that it is made worse by the destruction of large areas of rain forest and an increase in the world's *greenhouse gases* (e.g. carbon dioxide).

Hints and Tips!

A question that asks you to *compare* or say how something is *different* needs a link word like 'but' or 'whereas' in the answer.

Hints and Tips!

'Use news extracts' means you *must* quote evidence from the extract. The examiner will be looking for you to do so.

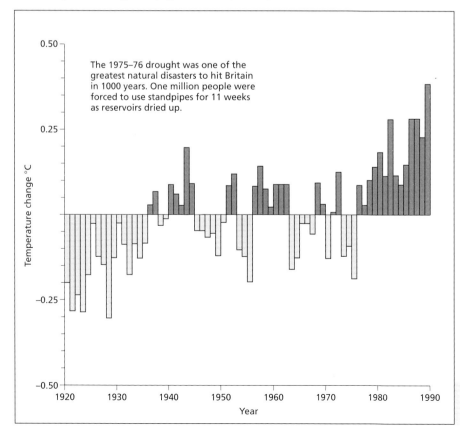

The 1975–76 drought was one of the greatest natural disasters to hit Britain in 1000 years. One million people were forced to use standpipes for 11 weeks as reservoirs dried up.

◀ *1.15 Temperature change*

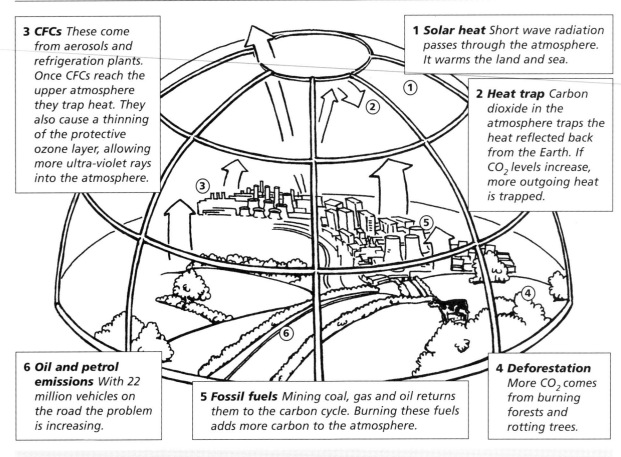

3 CFCs *These come from aerosols and refrigeration plants. Once CFCs reach the upper atmosphere they trap heat. They also cause a thinning of the protective ozone layer, allowing more ultra-violet rays into the atmosphere.*

1 Solar heat *Short wave radiation passes through the atmosphere. It warms the land and sea.*

2 Heat trap *Carbon dioxide in the atmosphere traps the heat reflected back from the Earth. If CO_2 levels increase, more outgoing heat is trapped.*

6 Oil and petrol emissions *With 22 million vehicles on the road the problem is increasing.*

5 Fossil fuels *Mining coal, gas and oil returns them to the carbon cycle. Burning these fuels adds more carbon to the atmosphere.*

4 Deforestation *More CO_2 comes from burning forests and rotting trees.*

▲ **1.16** *The greenhouse effect – should we be worried?*

Temperature changes are not new

Human activity is often blamed for global warming but it is not new. The Earth is over 4600 million years old. In that time it has been warmer with dry periods and cooler with ice sheets covering continents. These changes have taken place quite naturally without the influence of human activity.

What has caused concern in recent years have been the unusual weather and climate events reported in the media. Droughts, floods and hurricanes have affected places that are not used to such extreme weather.

Some of these changes are thought to be due to the activities of people rather than to nature alone.

Atlantic fishing grounds show increase in warm water fish

▲ **1.17** *What the papers say*

Hints and Tips!

'Use news extracts' means you *must* quote evidence from the extract. The examiner will be looking for you to do so.

Action Point

Use graph 1.15 on page 21 to describe the trend in temperature between 1920 and 1990. Use sketch 1.16 to list four causes of global warming. For two of these, explain how people's activities are causing the problem. Use the news reports 1.17 to describe one positive way in which the greenhouse effect is affecting people. Suggest two negative effects of the greenhouse effect on the environment.

How do ecosystems operate? (a)

Ecosystems are systems of links between plants and animals and the *habitats* in which they live. It is normal to show these natural environments as systems diagrams having inputs, outputs, stores and flows.

Ecosystems operate at a variety of scales, from local to global. They are a response to the climates in which they are found. Global ecosystems are called *biomes*.

▼ *1.18* The tropical rain forest biome

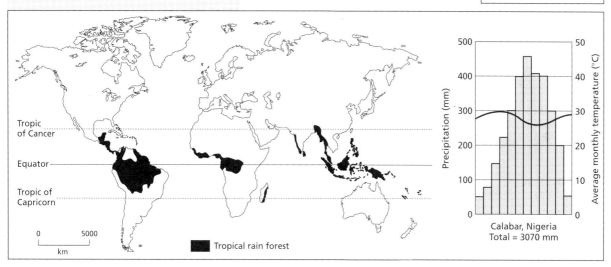

Calabar, Nigeria
Total = 3070 mm

Inputs: material or energy moving into the system.

Outputs: material or energy leaving the system.

Stores: places where material or energy is at rest.

Flows: movement of material or energy between stores.

The diagram below shows a simple systems diagram for the tropical rain forest.

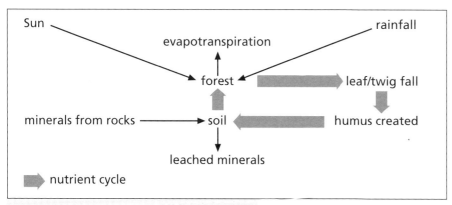

▲ *1.19* The tropical rain forest system

Action Point

Use map 1.18 to help you describe the distribution of the tropical rain forest (TRF). Use the climate graph to give two reasons why the TRF has a rich vegetation.

Action Point

Look at flow diagram 1.19.

List two inputs, two outputs and two stores in the rain forest.

Describe fully what happens to dead leaves and twigs in the system.

Hints and Tips!

When you are asked what happens to one item in the flow diagram, don't just state the obvious. You need to pick up 4 marks by describing fully the sequence of events that starts with dead twigs and leaves.

How do ecosystems operate? (b)

Plants and animals live within any ecosystem. The ways in which they relate to each other are shown in a *food web*. Within any food web are the following:

Producers: plants that fix energy from the Sun using photosynthesis.

Primary consumers: animals that eat plants – herbivores.

Secondary consumers: animals that eat other animals – carnivores.

Tertiary consumers: eat primary and secondary consumers.

This is complicated by the fact that some animals eat both plants and other animals – they are *omnivores*.

This relationship can again be shown as a diagram:

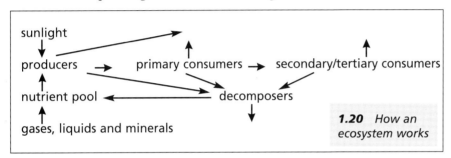

1.20 How an ecosystem works

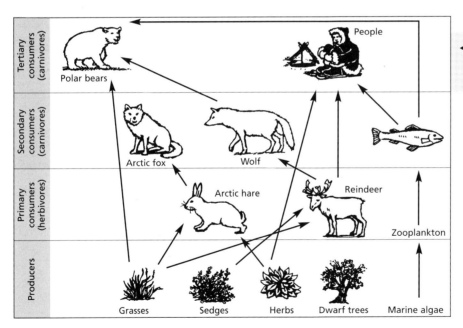

1.21 A rich variety of life exists in this tundra environment

How are ecosystems seen as a resource?

People have lived as part of ecosystems for centuries. Look at the position of the people in diagram 1.21. By being just one part of the ecosystem and only taking from the environment what they need for life, many groups of people still live in this way. They respect their environment and do not destroy it. Their lifestyle is sustainable. Within the tropical rain forests of Borneo, the Penan have a similar lifestyle.

Action Point

Look at flow diagram 1.20.

Name two outputs on the diagram that are arrowed but not named.

Describe the diagram in terms of flows, stores, inputs and outputs.

Action Point

Using flow diagram 1.21, of a tundra ecosystem, describe one food chain that has grasses as the producer. Explain what might happen if reindeer were removed from the food web.

Hints and Tips!

Removal of a producer or consumer from a food web. Remember that there are a number of effects that happen in sequence. In the case of reindeer, you should be looking first at its immediate effects on both the carnivores/omnivores and the producers. Then look for knock-on effects leading on from these.

Not long ago we were happy.
Things were good
Our fish was clean
Our food was pure

We live by getting palm heart, by getting sago
We eat different types of animals.
We are content making sago

There are many medicines,
many hunting poisons here in the forest.

If the land is preserved like this ...
all the animals happy to eat the fruit of the trees.
Satisfied life.
They eat the fruits.
We eat them.

We go out with blowpipe, get something return ... ah!
Content to eat, content with life.

This is a good life

▲ **1.22** *A Penan poem by Dawat Lupung*

Many ecosystems, like the rain forest, have in recent years been seen as a resource in a different way. Outsiders, especially 'Western' *multi-national companies* (MNCs) have moved in to log the forests. There are a number of features of logging by outsiders that apply to the exploitation of other environments around the world by big business:

- The loggers don't care – when they have finished they move on.
- They use heavy machinery that breaks up the soil.
- They pay very little to the real owners of the land to take their property.
- They do not replace what they take.
- They destroy many more trees than they take.

Action Point

Use poem 1.22.

List four materials the Penan take from the tropical rain forest.

Explain how the Penan rely on the forest for life.

Hints and Tips!

'Explain how the Penan ...' doesn't tell you how many ways you need to give, so that becomes your choice. Go for either simple ways or more detailed (So what?) statements.

◀ **1.23** *Reasons for rain forest destruction*

Action Point

Look at sketch 1.23.

List four reasons shown by the cartoons why rain forests are being destroyed.

Choose one that's probably the result of involvement by MNCs. Explain why the activity is taking place.

The effects of ecosystem destruction

Destruction like this has three sets of effects.

1 On the immediate environment

a The soil is exposed to the heavy rain.
b Rivers become polluted.
c Heavy machinery and dragging logs have destroyed the topsoil.
d Those nutrients that are left are removed by leaching.
e Rain washes soil particles into the rivers.

◄ **1.24** For every tree taken from the forest another 19 are destroyed

Action Point

Describe the scene in photo 1.24. Rearrange the statements a–e in order to show how removing trees damages the soil.

2 On the people living as part of the ecosystem

We don't like the company to destroy the forests any more; they make the water muddy, we become ill, we get TB, we get eye illness, we get malaria, we get killed on the bulldozer roads ...

There is not enough to eat. Many people will die – no food soon many people die.

The water muddy, the fish are dead. Can't drink the water any more, muddy, terrible, no good.

▲ **1.25** Thoughts of Dawat Lupung

Hints and Tips!

'Describe the scene ...' means just say what you see. You don't need to give reasons or opinions so you shouldn't use 'because'.

3 On the environment beyond the area of destruction

In some cases there is a knock-on effect of the destruction to places close to the area that has been destroyed. For example, when an area of rain forest is destroyed, large amounts of soil are washed into streams and rivers. This affects water quality and fish stock further downstream. Because the river bed receives a large amount of soil material, it also results in much more flooding than there was before.

Action Point

Read the poem in 1.25. Explain how logging has affected the traditional lives of the Penan.

And even wider effects

There are in many cases, though, effects that stretch far beyond the area of destruction and can be global in scale. Go back to the work you did on the 'greenhouse effect' on pages 21 and 22. What part does deforestation play in the greenhouse effect? What might be the effects of global warming on people living in the UK?

Hints and Tips!

You are asked to explain how logging affected the Penan so you must do more than just quote evidence from the poem.

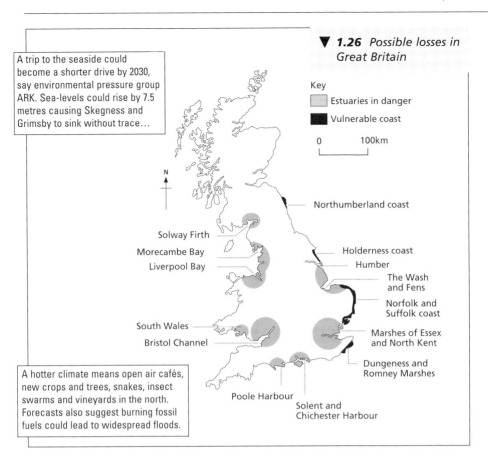

A trip to the seaside could become a shorter drive by 2030, say environmental pressure group ARK. Sea-levels could rise by 7.5 metres causing Skegness and Grimsby to sink without trace...

▼ 1.26 *Possible losses in Great Britain*

Key

Estuaries in danger

Vulnerable coast

0   100km

N

Northumberland coast

Solway Firth
Morecambe Bay
Liverpool Bay

Holderness coast
Humber
The Wash and Fens
Norfolk and Suffolk coast

South Wales
Bristol Channel

Marshes of Essex and North Kent

Dungeness and Romney Marshes

Poole Harbour

Solent and Chichester Harbour

A hotter climate means open air cafés, new crops and trees, snakes, insect swarms and vineyards in the north. Forecasts also suggest burning fossil fuels could lead to widespread floods.

Action Point

Look at map 1.26. Describe the distribution of areas in **Great Britain** that would suffer from a rise in sea level. Suggest ways in which people might react to these changes in sea level.

Action Point

Use diagram 1.27 to describe how each protection method works. Explain how each could help to sustainably develop the environment and economy of a country.

How might ecosystems be conserved?

The effects of ecosystem destruction are seen at a range of scales from local to global. These problems have been recognised in recent years and there have been a number of international conferences to reach agreement on solutions to the problems.

One major difficulty is managing, on one side, the desire to make profit out of the environment and, on the other, the need not to destroy it: in short, the need to exploit and also conserve. For many LEDCs the threatened environments are a means of helping solve their debt problems.

Medical research.

Some environments contain the possibility of cures for major illnesses. Pharmaceutical companies may be persuaded to put money into such areas to prevent them being destroyed.

Eco-tourism

is holiday-making that tries not to destroy the environments the tourists come to see. This can also bring money into areas under threat.

▶ 1.27 *Using biosphere reserves is one possible means of rain forest protection*

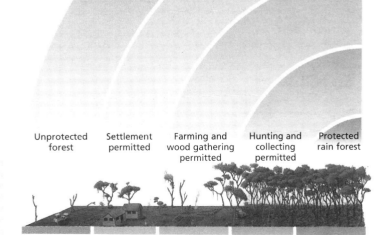

Unprotected forest

Settlement permitted

Farming and wood gathering permitted

Hunting and collecting permitted

Protected rain forest

Terms and meanings: Climate, the environment and people

Here are some important terms for you to match up and learn. The answers are at the back of the book – but don't cheat!

Term

1 Anticyclone

2 Biomes

3 Biosphere

4 Climate

5 Conserve

6 Depression

7 Desert

8 Ecosystem

9 Exploit

10 Humus

11 Leaching

12 Maximum temperature

13 Minimum temperature

14 Nutrients

15 Photosynthesis

16 Precipitation

17 Stewards

18 Sustainable

19 Synoptic chart

20 Temperate

21 Weather

Meaning

A A chemical reaction which results in nutrients in the soil being replaced by hydrogen from rainfall. Nutrients are lost or move deeper down the profile.

B A low pressure weather system formed in the mid-latitudes of the northern hemisphere where a tropical warm air mass pushes into an arctic cold air mass. Warm air rises to give low pressure at the centre of the weather system. This is usually less than 1000 millibars.

C People entrusted with the management of property, including the environment, to ensure it is useful to future generations.

D The average of weather conditions over a long period, at least thirty years. Temperature and precipitation are the most often used climate data and are shown on climate graphs.

E Capable, by careful use and management, of being maintained for future generations.

F Large ecosystems at the global scale where the climate and vegetation are uniform. Human activity may have destroyed or changed parts of the biome.

G Areas in the northern and southern hemispheres that do not experience great extremes of heat or cold. They are in the mid-latitudes between the hot tropics and cold polar regions.

H Decomposed organic material from dead plants and animals that forms the top layer or horizon of a soil and gives a brown colour to the soil, e.g. in a brown earth soil.

I A system of links between plants and animals (the living community) and the habitats where they live, including the non-living environment.

J The highest temperature recorded during a time period. This is usually during a 24-hour period but can be monthly or yearly.

K The movement of water from the air to the Earth's surface in forms such as rain, snow, hail, frost and dew.

L To use the natural environment as a resource and to make a profit.

M An area having annual precipitation of less than 250mm a year.

N A map that gives the general view of the weather over a large area for a short period of time.

O The regions of the Earth and atmosphere where plants and animals live.

P Materials which plants use for food.

Q To prevent an environment being damaged by exploitation, or to repair an environment that has already been damaged.

R The process whereby plants take in the Sun's energy with carbon dioxide and water to produce energy, oxygen and plant tissue.

S The lowest temperature recorded during a time period. This is usually during a 24-hour period but can be monthly or yearly.

T A high pressure weather system. Average sea-level pressure at the centre of the system is usually above 1000 millibars.

U Short-term, day-to-day changes in the atmosphere. Weather recording usually includes rainfall, temperature, cloud cover, and wind speed and direction.

Unit 2: Water, landforms and people

How does the hydrological cycle operate?

The whole of this unit is based on the hydrological cycle which operates within the *hydrosphere*. It consists of all the stores and flows of water in its gas, liquid and solid states. When rain falls it takes various routes back to the oceans and, eventually, the atmosphere. This whole circle or cycle of water movement may be shown as a *systems diagram*. Water *flows* between stores in the hydrological cycle.

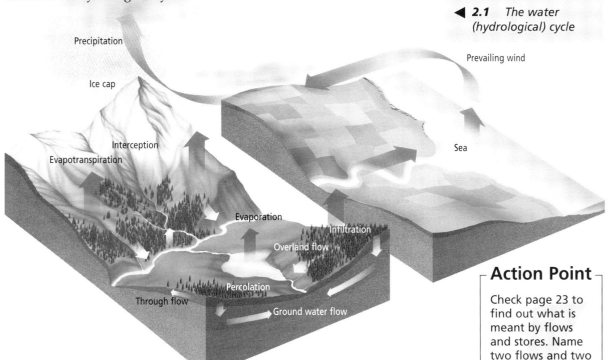

◀ *2.1 The water (hydrological) cycle*

Precipitation

Ice cap

Interception

Evapotranspiration

Evaporation

Infiltration

Overland flow

Percolation

Through flow

Ground water flow

Prevailing wind

Sea

Action Point

Check page 23 to find out what is meant by flows and stores. Name two flows and two stores in diagram 2.1. Describe what happens to water after it has been evaporated from the sea.

A river basin or drainage basin is also called a *catchment* area. It is divided from other river basins by a *watershed*. Within a river basin the main river is fed by tributaries and the water finally enters the sea or a lake at the river's mouth. This is sometimes called an *estuary*. These are shown in this simple diagram.

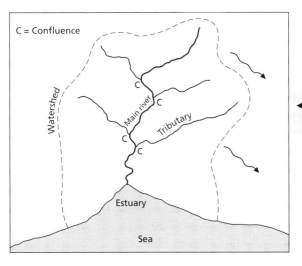

C = Confluence

Watershed

Main river

Tributary

Estuary

Sea

◀ *2.2 A model drainage basin*

Hints and Tips!

Remember that water that has evaporated from the sea will eventually reach the sea again.

What you can't see on the river basin diagram is everything that happens to the water after it falls on the river basin. It only shows the *surface* flow of water. The movement of water in a river basin can also be shown in a systems diagram. As well as flows and stores, this diagram has *inputs* and *outputs*.

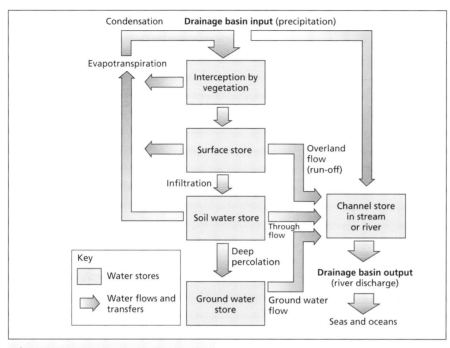

▲ **2.3** *Not all water follows a direct route back to the sea. There are other ways ...*

People interfere with the flow of water in a river basin. For example, by removing trees they can alter the flow of water. There would be:

Effects and Reasons

E Less transpiration
R There are fewer trees to give off water.

E Faster surface flow
R There is less interception by trees.

E Less infiltration
R Pores in the soil cannot cope with the large amounts of water arriving at the same time.

E Greater flood risk
R Water arrives in the rivers quicker. It also erodes soil and deposits it on the river bed.

Building dams also alters water flow.

2.4 *People can change water cycles*

> **Action Point**
>
> Name one input, one output, two flows and two stores in flow diagram 2.3.
>
> Describe the routes taken by water that falls on the trees (vegetation) in the diagram.

> **Action Point**
>
> Explain how building the dam in diagram 2.4 will have affected:
>
> • river flow
>
> • water storage
>
> • evaporation.

> *Hints and Tips!*
>
> You are now being asked to *explain*. You should use words like 'because'.

The flow of water in urban areas is completely different to that in rural areas. Very little water here infiltrates the ground. Much of it falls onto concrete or tarmac surfaces or buildings and is taken by drainage pipes very quickly to the river.

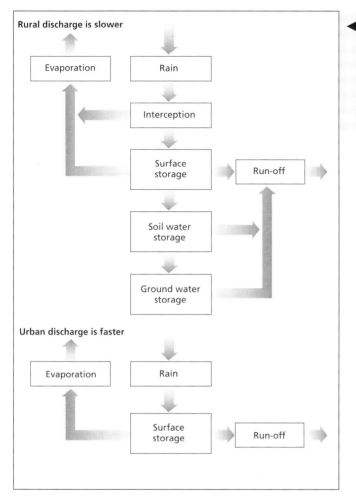

◀ *2.5* *The rate at which rainfall reaches a river will influence discharge rates*

Graph 2.6 is used to answer the exam practice question on page 33. Attempt it now. Precipitation is shown using a bar graph, and discharge is shown using a line graph.

Action Point

Describe water discharge in an urban area. Compare this with rural discharge.

Hints and Tips!

You are asked only to *describe* water discharge. You are not asked to explain it.

What is flooding?

If water flows down the river channel at a rate that is too fast for the channel to cope with, flooding occurs. *Bankfull stage* is the height of the water when the river channel can hold no more water. The flow of water in a river channel is its run-off (*discharge rate*) and is measured in cubic metres per second (cumecs) of water flowing past a particular point on the river. The relationship between rainfall and discharge rate is shown on a *flood hydrograph*.

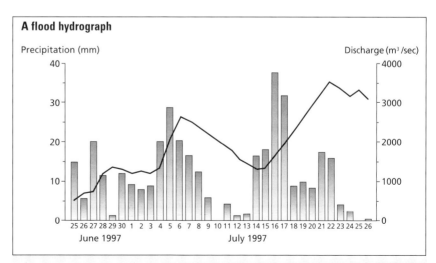

▲ *2.6* *Rainfall and run-off in the Oder Valley, June–July 1997. The flooding caused severe disruption to services, and damage to property and the environment in both Germany and Poland.*

Flooding has many causes. They are usually a combination of the effects of nature and the activities of people.

Natural causes:
- very heavy rainfall
- an already high water table
- rapid snow melt
- many tributaries feeding main river
- frozen ground.

Hints and Tips!

When using graphs and other similar resources, make sure that you measure accurately. When describing patterns on graphs, state whether it is a rise or fall, give the rate of change, and quote figures/dates from the graph.

▲ **2.7** *Some natural causes of flooding*

Human causes:
- deforestation – this could be the deliberate chopping down of trees or their destruction by acid rain
- draining farmland higher up the river
- creation of urban areas.

▼ **2.8** *Some human causes of flooding*

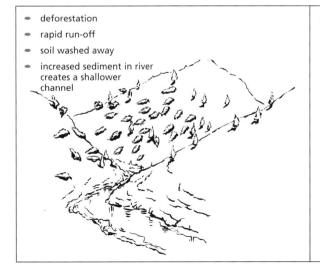

- deforestation
- rapid run-off
- soil washed away
- increased sediment in river creates a shallower channel

- water falls on buildings and tarmac
- runs down drains and is channelled quickly to river

There are a number of effects of flooding. It can affect people, their property, and wildlife. People can deal with flooding in a number of ways. Some of these methods prevent flooding happening. Others protect people and property when flooding occurs.

Action Point

Explain how either deforestation or artificial drainage could help cause flooding.

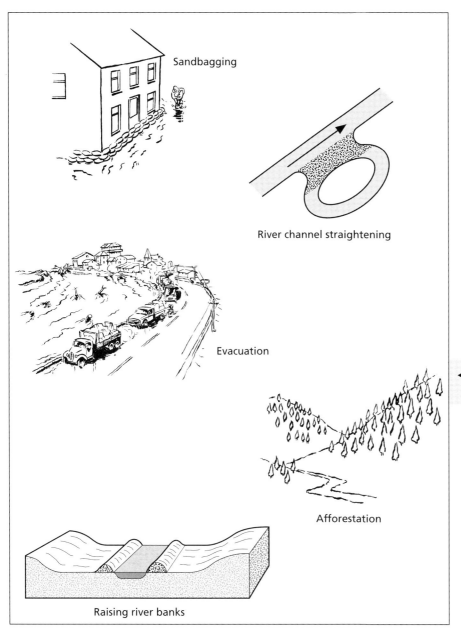

Sandbagging

River channel straightening

Evacuation

Afforestation

Raising river banks

Action Point

Describe the three effects of flooding shown in photos C, D and E in the colour resources section. Suggest problems the man in photo C may face when the flood waters go down.

◀ **2.9** *Protection against flooding*

Action Point

List the following as either flood prevention or flood protection methods:

sandbagging; river channel straightening; afforestation; evacuation; raising of river banks.

Choose two flood prevention methods. Explain how they work.

Exam practice

Look at Graph 2.6 on page 31 of this revision guide.

(a) When was peak rainfall? (1 mark)

(b) How long was the delay between peak rainfall and peak runoff? (1 mark)

(c) Describe the pattern of discharge between 10 and 24 of July (3 marks)

(d) Give two reasons for the delay between peak rainfall and peak discharge. (4 marks)

Providing a sustainable water supply

Water is essential to life. Although enough fresh water falls across the world for all our needs, it does not always fall where and when we need it. Water storage and transfer is essential to distributing water effectively. Water is mainly stored in surface reservoirs and underground in porous rocks like chalk and sandstone.

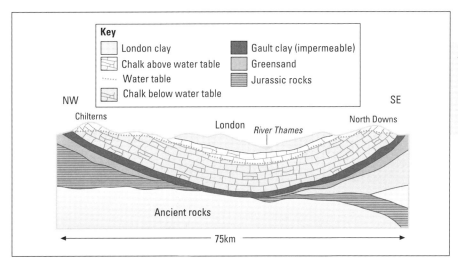

◀ **2.10** *Much of London's water traditionally comes from underground sources*

Surface water is often stored behind dams. Many of these are multi-purpose dams. They may control flooding, save water for irrigating farmland and transfer to cities and industrial areas, and generate hydro-electric power. The creation of a reservoir may also bring new work, recreation and food opportunities.

The site of a new reservoir requires careful consideration.

The ideal site would have:	Reasons (jumbled)
1 A steep-sided, narrow valley	A so little compensation would be paid
2 Impermeable rocks	B so the water volume is large compared with the surface area
3 Dense vegetation cover	C so used water is constantly replaced
4 High annual rainfall	D so little water is lost through leaking pipes
5 Low air temperatures	E so water is intercepted, avoiding soil erosion and reservoir silting
6 Low land values	F so little water is lost through infiltration
7 Low population density	G so little water is lost through evaporation
8 A short distance to the user	H so few people will need to be rehoused

Large rivers may cross international boundaries, so international co-operation is often required when considering the building of new dams. For example, a new dam across the River Nile in Sudan could cause major problems for the people of Egypt.

Hints and Tips!

Useful terms like *aquifer* and *water table* are found in the list of 'Terms and meanings' on page 42.

Action Point

What is meant by *aquifer* and *water table*? Which rock is London's aquifer? What problems might London experience if the water table rose considerably? What would be the effect if it lowered a great deal?

Know your Case Study

Using information from a Case Study you have used, explain how a new reservoir may provide work, recreation and food opportunities.

Action Point

Use the table on this page to match the features of the site of an ideal reservoir to the reasons why each feature is important.

What is drought?

Drought is not simply low rainfall. Some parts of the world always receive a low rainfall. This is expected and people in these areas live according to the small amounts of rain they expect. Examples include the pastoral nomads who inhabit the world's hot deserts and who follow their herds of animals in search of pasture. Drought occurs when a great deal less rain falls than is expected in an area.

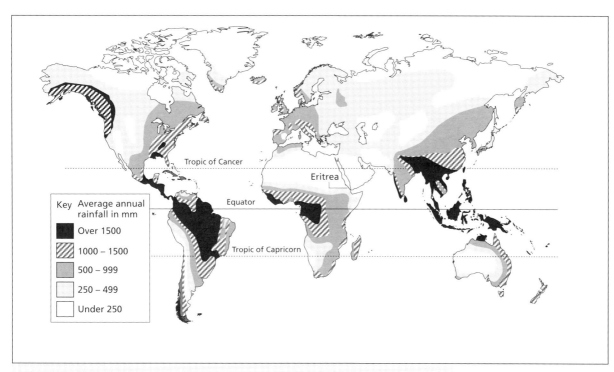

▲ **2.11** *Wet and dry areas of the world*

Every day 60-year-old Lemlem Weldnkil makes a three-hour round trip from her home down a steep, rocky hillside to the nearest water which is dirty and used by animals. Carrying her daily ration of 20 litres is exhausting. She knows the water could make her family ill.

◀ **2.12** *Access to water in rural Eritrea*

In many Less Economically Developed Countries (LEDCs) it has proven very difficult to do anything when drought happens. Suffering on the southern edge of the Sahara Desert in the Sahel has been a feature of the last twenty years. Crops do not grow, people starve and aid agencies from More Economically Developed Countries (MEDCs) try to save people's lives, often by giving emergency aid. Countries like Eritrea have been badly affected in recent years.

Action Point

Use map 2.11.
(a) What is the annual rainfall of Eritrea?
(b) Describe the distribution of areas of low rainfall.

What is needed is a longer-term means of stopping the effects of drought. Sustainable routes to development are those that can be continued by the people without outside help in the future.

> For Fesehaye the new water supply itself can be a source of income. In his village of Adisheka in Eritrea he earns a living as a tapstand attendant, looking after the community's two water fountains. Each fountain has four taps which need maintenance. Fesehaye opens one in the morning, the other in the afternoon. He charges 5 cents for every 20 litres and this fee is divided between Fesehaye's salary and the village fund to maintain the taps.

▲ **2.13** Access to water in an Eritrean village

Action Point

Read texts 2.12 and 2.13. Describe Fesehaye's job. Explain how his work could affect his quality of life and that of people like Lemlem.

How does water shape the land?

There is a difference between weathering and erosion. *Weathering* occurs when rock material is broken down but is not carried away. *Erosion* involves the breaking down of material and its removal.

▼ **2.14** Weathering: a carved figure on the roof of St Paul's Cathedral, London

▼ **2.15** Erosion: a fast-flowing stream in the Canadian Rockies

Rivers and seas are *agents of erosion*. Whichever of these agents is operating, the same three processes take place:

Erosion: the wearing away and removal of rock material.

Transport: the moving of eroded material to a different place.

Deposition: the dumping of transported material.

Whether along the course of rivers or at the coast, the same four processes of erosion take place:
- hydraulic action (quarrying)
- abrasion (corrasion)
- corrosion (solution)
- attrition.

Action Po

Use the list of 'Terms and meanings' on page 42 to work out what is meant by each of these processes of erosion.

After the material has been eroded it is transported by the energy of moving water. Rivers transport material downstream, and the sea transports it along the shore. The material being transported is the *load*. There are four types of load:
- **Solution load:** material that is dissolved in the water.
- **Suspension load:** material that is 'floating' in the water.
- **Saltation load:** material that is bounced along by the water.
- **Traction load:** material that is rolled along by the water.

Material is deposited when water slows down and loses its energy.

Hints and Tips!

Remember that if erosion and the landforms it produces are found in the exam paper, you may not have done *that* particular example. Just apply the basic principle in your answers.

Rivers

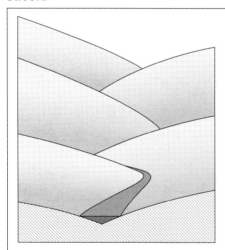 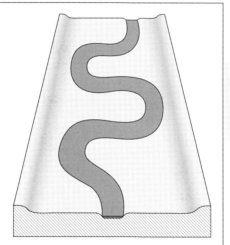

◀ **2.16** Upland and lowland river valleys: features of erosion and deposition

An upland river valley. In the upland valley the stream flows quickly over steep ground. The main process is vertical erosion. The river flows around obstacles creating interlocking spurs. Weathering processes wear back the valley sides as the stream erodes vertically, so a V-shaped valley is formed.

A lowland river valley. In the lowland valley the river flows more slowly over more level ground. It often meanders across a wide flood plain. The valley is wide due to lateral erosion of the valley sides. Deposition is the major process at the time of flooding, creating a very flat flood plain.

Action Point

Make copies of the diagrams 2.16, and then use evidence from the text to add labels showing the main features of the two valleys. Using another colour, annotate your diagram to explain how each valley forms.

The flood plain created in many lower river valleys has positive and negative impacts on people.

Positive impacts	Negative impacts
Flat land suitable for farming	Frequent flood hazard
Fertile silt deposited each year	Soil often too wet and heavy for ploughing
Easy transport routes	

The Nile flood plain and delta supported one of the world's greatest early civilisations. Today 3% of Egypt's land supports almost all of its population; the rest is hot desert.

The Aswan Dam was built in southern Egypt in 1964. It is a multi-purpose scheme that has many benefits for the people of Egypt. Not all effects have been good, though, and the Nile delta is now suffering. The effects could be made even worse by the effects of global warming and a predicted rise in the level of the Mediterranean Sea.

Action Point

Use evidence from map 2.17 to explain how the activities of people can starve the delta of sediment. Suggest how this might put the delta in danger from the Mediterranean Sea.

Use maps 2.18 to describe possible future changes on the delta. Suggest how this may affect the people of Egypt.

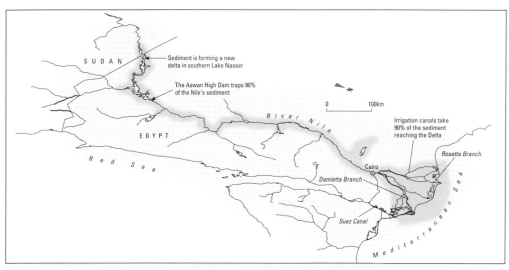

▲ **2.17** *Effects of building the Aswan Dam*

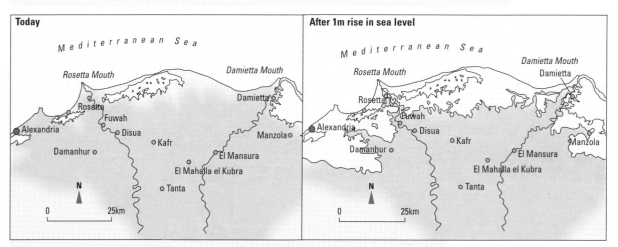

▲ **2.18** *A disappearing delta?*

Coasts

The rate at which a coast erodes depends on the resistance to erosion of the rock material from which it is formed. Less resistant (soft) rock erodes quickly and tends to produce bays in which rock material slumps down the cliffs and is rapidly transported away. Where the rock is more resistant, headlands are formed.

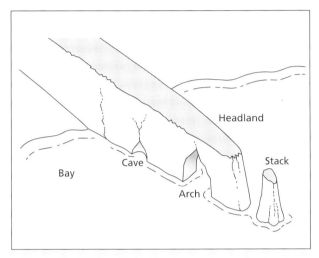

▲ **2.19** *Cliff erosion: landforms and processes.*

▲ **2.20** *A headland at Etretat on the north coast of France*

Movement along the coast is called *longshore drift*. It is the result of the operation of two processes:

1 Water carries beach material up the shore. This is the *swash* and is controlled by the direction of wave movement.
2 When the wave has broken, water drags the beach material back at right-angles to the shore. This is called *backwash*.

Action Point

Use information from diagram 2.19 to label a copy of photo 2.20, to show the main features of the headland. Annotate your sketch to show how these features formed.

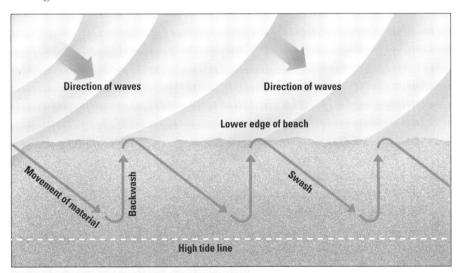

▲ **2.21** *How longshore drift operates*

Material transported by longshore drift normally forms beaches. When the direction of the shore changes, or when it is interrupted by a large river estuary, a *spit* may be formed.

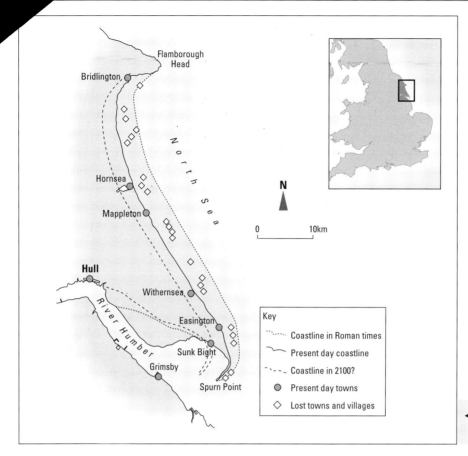

Action Point

Use information from map 2.22 and photo M in the colour resources section to describe how Spurn Point is being used by people. Explain how this feature formed.

Know your Case Study

Describe how a river landform you have studied was formed. Explain how it is used by people.

◀ **2.22** *The changing Holderness coast*

A problem-solving activity: Should the Holderness coast be protected?

The Holderness coast is mainly composed of low cliffs made of boulder clay. This material was deposited about 10 000 years ago as the ice melted at the end of the last glaciation. It is a crumbly rock that has very little resistance to erosion. Erosion is so rapid that, in some places, the land is disappearing at a rate of over half a metre a year.

Action Point

Use map 2.22 to describe the location of the Holderness coast. How has it eroded since Roman times? Describe how it is expected to erode in the next 100 years.

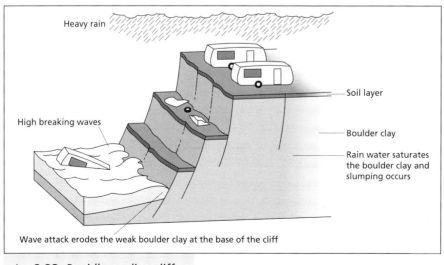

Heavy rain

Soil layer

High breaking waves

Boulder clay

Rain water saturates the boulder clay and slumping occurs

Wave attack erodes the weak boulder clay at the base of the cliff

▲ **2.23** *Rapidly eroding cliffs*

Action Point

Describe the erosion shown in diagram 2.23. Explain the processes of erosion that are operating on the cliff.

How might the coast be protected?

If the coast is not protected, it will continue to erode at the present rate, and the result is likely to be the coastline shown for 2100 on map 2.22, on page 40. There are several ways in which parts of the coast might be protected. Some of these are shown in figure 2.24. Protecting the whole coastline is very expensive, and not an option. Among other places, the small village of Mappleton has been protected using rock armour and rock groynes. The cliffs here have been graded. In contrast, the holiday resort of Withernsea has a concrete sea wall, protected by rock armour and a series of wooden groynes.

Hard engineering involves placing structures along the coast that are designed to prevent erosion. It may be expensive, as with the sea wall, or relatively cheap, as with rock armour. Groynes prevent the movement of sand and build up the beach.

Soft engineering mainly involves the placing of beach material in front of the cliff. The wave energy is absorbed by the beach and not the cliff. Sand is usually dredged from further offshore.

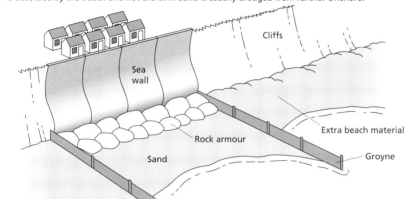

◀ **2.24** *Coastal protection methods*

FOR PROTECTION

Mappleton resident
Before protection, the average erosion rate was 2 metres a year. By 1988 my bedroom was 8 metres from the cliff edge. Since the scheme was put in place there has been no more erosion.

Withernsea shopkeeper
Occasionally the sea wall is breached, but it is then repaired. Although not as popular as in the past, we still get many summer visitors and the town is a retirement centre.

AGAINST PROTECTION

Cowden resident
We could cope with the erosion as it was before the the Mappleton protection scheme was put in place. Now, erosion is much faster than previously and our settlement is disappearing into the sea at an alarming rate.

BP spokesperson
We have a terminal at Easington where North Sea gas comes ashore. The cliffs are dangerously close and the villagers want a 1.6 km stretch of coast protected. The 700 residents believe that the village will be destroyed if the scheme supported by government to protect only the 1 km in front of the gas terminal goes ahead.

▲ **2.25** *What do people think?*

The effect of ... protection	Hard protection	Soft protection	Do nothing
... on people in protected areas			
... on people in unprotected areas			

Action Point

Look at figure 2.24. How do soft and hard protection methods compare in terms of protection and their effects on other parts of the coast?

Action Point

Use figure 2.24 to help you explain the views of people in favour of, and against, protecting parts of the Holderness coast.

Action Point

It's your decision. How would *you* plan for this area of coast in the future? Should new areas be protected, or not? Write a letter stating what should be done, and justifying your choice of strategy. Use a large copy of the table (left) to help you organise your ideas.

Terms and meanings: Water, landforms and people

Here are some important terms for you to match up and learn. The answers are at the back of the book – but don't cheat!

Term

1 Abrasion

2 Agent of erosion

3 Aquifer

4 Attrition

5 Bankfull stage

6 Corrosion

7 Deposition

8 Differential erosion

9 Discharge

10 Erosion

11 Flood plain

12 Hydrosphere

13 Impermeable

14 Input

15 Irrigation

16 Porous

17 Transport

18 Water (hydrological) cycle

19 Water deficit

20 Water table

21 Weathering

Meaning

A A rock structure that will hold water. Water can be abstracted from the rock by drilling boreholes.

B The artificial supply of water to land by such means as channels, sprinklers and hosepipes.

C The uneven erosion of relatively hard and soft rocks. It is responsible for such features as waterfalls, and headlands and bays scenery.

D The constant recycling of water between the atmosphere and the Earth's surface.

E The wearing away of rock fragments as they rub against each other during transportation.

F The wearing away and removal of rock material by the action of such agents as wind, water and ice.

G Rocks that do not allow water to pass through them. The opposite of *permeable*, which are rocks that do allow water to pass through them.

H A deficit exists when water supply is lower than demand. The opposite of a water surplus where water supply is greater than demand.

I Erosion which takes place when a rock material, such as limestone, is dissolved and carried in solution by water.

J All the stores and flows of water in its gas, liquid and solid states.

K The dumping of eroded material in the place that it has been transported to.

L The movement of eroded material from the place of erosion to the place in which it is deposited.

M Material that is put in or taken into a system. Water as precipitation is the input to a drainage basin.

N The eroding away of rock surfaces by pieces of rock held in rivers, sea, ice and wind. Also known as corrasion.

O The level below which the ground is saturated with water. It usually varies according to the season.

P A form of permeable rock in which the water passes through pores in the rock.

Q The volume of water flowing across the width of a river at a given point. It is measured in cubic metres per second (cumecs).

R A force responsible for wearing away the Earth's surface.

S A stretch of relatively flat land on the sides of a river. It is usually covered by fertile flood deposits called alluvium.

T The breakdown of rocks without their removal.

U The discharge at which a river is level with the top of its banks and is about to flood.

Unit 3: People and place

How and why does an area's population change with time?

There are some easy and some not so easy answers to this question. In simple terms, the population of an area or region can either remain the same, decline or grow. It is the reasons for these changes that bring in complications! Changes are due to:

1 natural increase and decrease
2 migration.

Natural changes in population size will reflect relationships between birth rates and death rates:

- If the birth rate is greater than the death rate, there will be a natural increase in population.
- If the death rate is greater than the birth rate, there will be a natural decrease in population.

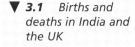

▼ **3.1** *Births and deaths in India and the UK*

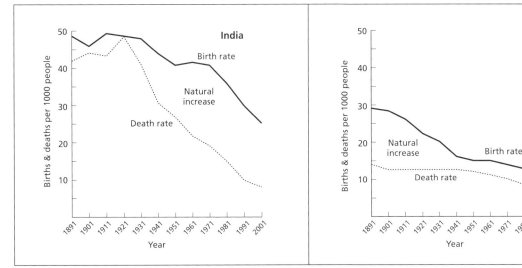

The reasons for different birth and death rates are many but they are mainly related to the degree of economic development found within a country or region. We have seen that India (an LEDC) has a much greater natural increase in population than the UK. Although it is a popular idea that the differences are all the result of having or not having access to birth control or the education to use it, such an idea is far too simple. The reasons for a large natural increase in population in LEDCs are quite varied:

- Infant mortality rates are high, *so* parents want large families as only a few children may survive to become adults.
- In rural communities many people are needed on the land, *so* a large family ensures a labour force without needing to employ labourers.
- Some religions ban the practice of birth control, *so* people who follow that religion are likely to have large families.

Action Point

Look at graphs 3.1. Describe the birth rate for India between 1891 and 2001. Compare India's death rate with its birth rate. In what ways are changes in the UK's population different from those in India?

Add to all these the effects of improved healthcare and a lower death rate, and a large natural increase of population is the result.

There is, though, evidence within many LEDC countries that large families are a feature of the countryside and that families living in urban areas are, on average, much smaller.

What all this means in terms of a country's population structure is shown below:

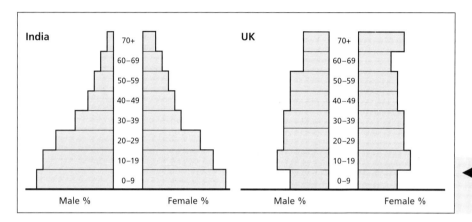

◀ **3.2** *Population pyramids for India and the UK*

! Action Point

Decide which of the following pairs of statements applies to an MEDC and which to an LEDC:

A high birth rate gives a wide base.	A low birth rate gives a narrow base.
Low infant mortality and a low death rate give steep sides.	High infant mortality and a high death rate give near vertical sides.
A high life expectancy gives a wide top.	A low life expectancy gives a narrow top.

What are the main patterns of migration and why do they take place?

Migration is the movement of people from one area to another.

Migration may be:
- permanent or temporary
- forced or voluntary
- internal or international.

Migration is also the other reason for changes in the population of an area. When there is a large movement of people into or out of an area, it will have a marked effect on population structures.

Each individual person or family that moves does so for reasons that are unique, but there are some general ideas and principles that go a long way towards explaining why people move. These may be divided into:

Push factors – features of the place in which a person is living that are seen as reasons for moving away from that place.
Pull factors – what the migrant thinks or has heard about the destination place will be like. These are attractions of the place that, sometimes, are not true in reality.

The general movements experienced in LEDCs and MEDCs tend to be different and have their own push and pull factors.

Urbanisation: the LEDC story

A feature of recent years in most LEDCs has been a movement of people from rural to urban areas: from the countryside to the cities.

▼ **3.3**   The distribution of the world's largest cities is changing

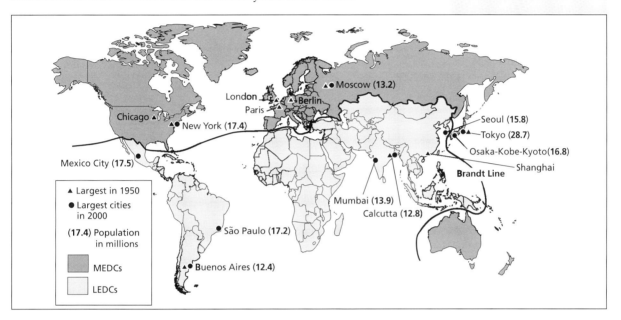

Legend:
▲ Largest in 1950
● Largest cities in 2000
(17.4) Population in millions

MEDCs
LEDCs

City labels:
Moscow **(13.2)**
London
Paris
Berlin
Chicago
New York **(17.4)**
Mexico City **(17.5)**
Seoul **(15.8)**
Tokyo **(28.7)**
Osaka-Kobe-Kyoto **(16.8)**
Shanghai
Brandt Line
Mumbai **(13.9)**
Calcutta **(12.8)**
São Paulo **(17.2)**
Buenos Aires **(12.4)**

What pushes people away from the countryside?

Every individual who moves has his or her own unique reasons for moving. These are some of the more common reasons:

- Farmland in many countries is, on the death of the farmer, inherited by the eldest son. Others have no land and so must move.
- The area is hit by drought or flooding so people who are starving move.
- Many villages are isolated and have no health service, schools or education facilities, so people have a low quality of life.

Action Point

Use map 3.3 to describe the distribution of the world's largest cities in 1950. Compare the distribution of the world's largest cities in 1950 with that in 2000.

◄ **3.4**   The push of the countryside

What pulls people to the cities?

People in the countryside have the perception that:
- there is better healthcare, so there is a greater chance of survival
- there is the chance of education, so the children can train for better jobs
- there are jobs for everyone in the city, so there is the prospect of a regular wage
- the city is an exciting place to be, with entertainment and a great social life.

◀ **3.5** *The pull of the city*

It is often the case that people who migrate to the city already have relatives there who will look after them.

If large numbers of people migrate from an area of countryside or a single village, there could be a serious effect on the area they are leaving. It is usually the young and fit people who migrate and it is possible that a negative multiplier may set in:

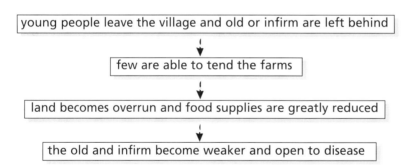

young people leave the village and old or infirm are left behind
↓
few are able to tend the farms
↓
land becomes overrun and food supplies are greatly reduced
↓
the old and infirm become weaker and open to disease

Living in an LEDC city

All cities are different but LEDC cities do seem to have a common land use pattern:

Centre	The Central Business District
↓	High-quality housing
↓	Low-quality housing
Suburbs	Squatter settlements

Zones of industry may be found cutting across these areas. They are found along main roads, railways and rivers. Squatter settlements are often found close to industrial areas and along lines of communication.

Exam practice

(a) Describe the housing in the foreground of photo 3.7 on page 47.
    (3 marks)

(b) How is the housing in the background different from that in the foreground?
    (4 marks)

(c) Which housing offers the best opportunities for a high quality of life? Explain your choice.
    (4 marks)

! Action Point

Reasons for the pattern of land use include:
- The main offices are found in the CBD and well-paid office workers do not wish to travel far to work.
- Many migrants arrive in the city by road and rail looking for a place to build a house.
- The rich do not wish to be troubled by poorer members of society so the city authorities move newcomers and the homeless out of the centre.
- Factories need transport routes to distribute their products, and water for their manufacturing processes.

Which land use feature of an LEDC city do each of these help to explain?

▼ *3.6 The location of Mumbai*

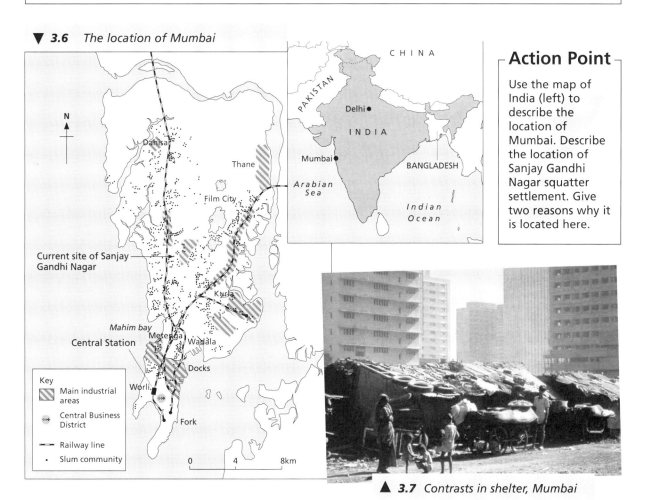

Action Point

Use the map of India (left) to describe the location of Mumbai. Describe the location of Sanjay Gandhi Nagar squatter settlement. Give two reasons why it is located here.

▲ *3.7 Contrasts in shelter, Mumbai*

! Action Point

Compare the two types of housing shown in photo 3.7. List differences you would expect to find inside the houses.

Hints and Tips!

The first question only asks you to compare what you see. It does not ask you to explain anything – don't use 'because' at this point – that comes in the second question!

Many of the houses in Sanjay Gandhi Nagar are similar to those in the foreground of photo 3.7. The whole squatter settlement is a mixture of houses and other buildings. Only a few of these are shown on the map below and, although less than in many squatter settlements, the housing density is high. Sanjay Gandhi Nagar has quite definite boundaries on all sides.

Most squatter settlements suffer from a number of problems:
- Houses are tightly packed together and housing density is high so there is a feeling of overcrowding.
- Many services are missing. There is poor access to running water and little sewerage, so disease spreads easily.
- There is no electricity supply so it is dark in the evenings and there is no TV for entertainment.
- There is little healthcare so infant mortality is high and life expectancy is low.
- People mainly have informal jobs so money earned is low and unreliable.
- The settlement location is undesirable and may be next to main roads or rail lines, so dangerous, or close to rivers, so regularly flood.

▼ **3.8** *A plan of the new site of Sanjay Gandhi Nagar*

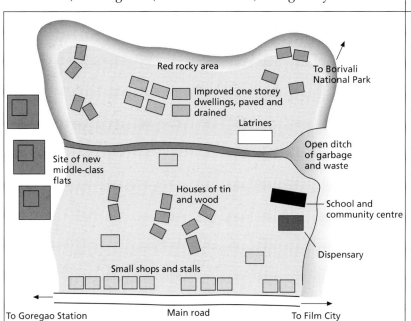

- There are permanent stores, shops and restaurants.
- The little streets are neat and most houses are very clean.
- The quarry used for housing stone is now half-filled with waste covered with bright green algae.
- Garbage dumps attract flies and mosquitoes. The council use a liquid pesticide.
- Public toilets are close to the houses.
- Houses are well spaced and housing density, at 300 families to a hectare, is low for slum communities.
- There is an area of open space in the centre.
- The electricity supply, paid for by the Residents' Association, is unreliable.
- Water taps only operate between 2:00am and 5:00am. Women fill any containers they can for that day's supply.

A problem-solving activity

When decisions are made about changes to a settlement or a part of a city, many different individuals and groups of people have opinions about what should happen. In Sanjay Gandhi Nagar the main groups are:
- the Maharashtra State Government
- the Mumbai municipal authorities
- the people of Sanjay Gandhi Nagar.

This list is written with the most powerful first. It is often the case that the people who have to live in an area have the least say in its future. This may change if they are capable of organising themselves, or get outside help. In Sanjay Gandhi Nagar, both of these have happened:
- The people have formed a Residents' Association. It takes decisions about such things as housing density, and how houses may be sold. It also runs some services.

Action Point

Use the map 3.8 to describe the boundaries of Sanjay Gandhi Nagar. List the services found in the settlement and explain how each may affect the quality of life of the residents.

- The community is helped by a Non-Government Organisation (NGO) called Navara Hakk. It has influential members and represents the community when decisions are made.

There are several ways in which Sanjay Gandhi Nagar could develop in future:

1 The authorities have suggested knocking down the whole settlement and replacing it with high-rise flats, some of which would be given to the residents and the others sold to outsiders. *Advantages* to the residents: they would own their own permanent home; they could sell it and return to the countryside. *Disadvantages*: they don't trust the developers; many residents couldn't afford the services provided with the flats.

2 The residents could be provided with cheap materials to build permanent homes with a water supply, sewerage and electricity. The residents would be expected to pay a very small sum for the materials and to build the houses themselves. In Sanjay Gandhi Nagar they already have the land, but if this was happening in a new settlement where the people were also being given the land, it would be called a 'site and service' scheme. *Advantages* to the residents: they would not have to move off their plot of land; costs to them would be low and mainly affordable; helping each other build the houses would unite the community. *Disadvantages*: not all can afford the costs involved; just improving the houses does not improve the general service provision to the community.

3 One option is to do nothing at all and allow the people living in the settlement to improve their houses as and when they can afford it. *Advantages* to residents: nobody is put in the position of paying for improvements they cannot afford; many residents do not like change. *Disadvantages*: the health problems remain; individual residents cannot bring in water supply and sewerage; improvements to only some houses would lead to a breakdown in the community spirit.

4 The whole community could be provided with more services, such as improved healthcare and education. *Advantages* to the residents: this would reduce infant mortality and improve life expectancy. *Disadvantages*: these services would have to be paid for and many residents could not afford them.

Action Point

Look at map 3.10 on page 51. Describe the location of the City Challenge area.

Action Point

You have been asked by the Residents' Association to suggest how the settlement of Sanjay Gandhi Nagar could be developed for the future. The development must meet the needs of the residents in that it improves quality of life and also improves work opportunities for the people living in the settlement. Show your development on a copy of the plan and write a letter to the Residents' Association justifying your choice of strategies.
A writing frame has been provided on page 81 to help you organise your letter. Within your letter make sure that you use 'So what?' statements. A similar writing frame could be used whenever you are asked to explain or justify the decisions you have made in the problem-solving paper.

Living in an MEDC city

The MEDC city is said to show definite patterns of land use. A number of models have been suggested but in its simplest form it is the reverse of that seen in LEDCs:

Centre	The Central Business District
↓	The inner city – an area of old houses and industry that is being re-developed
	Medium-cost housing
Suburbs	High-cost housing

The pattern is the result of the way in which the city has grown. Most cities in the UK and other European countries were small until the Industrial Revolution. In the UK this happened during the nineteenth century. Large numbers of workers moved into cities and small terraced houses were built to accommodate them close to the factories. The richer managers had houses built along main roads leading into the cities and as more houses were built, they filled the gaps between these. The large and expensive houses on the edges of cities reflect the idea that people do not now want to live close to their places of work and that both public and private transport are readily available and fairly cheap. The growth of council housing estates complicates this simple pattern, and many are found in the suburbs.

Contrasts in housing

3.9 *From the CBD to the suburbs*

Inner city: owner occupier
To buy: £42 250
To rent: £25 per week

Flats: owner occupier
To buy: £24 950
To rent: £55 per week

Large detached: owner occupier
To buy: £127 750
To rent: £100 per week

Suburbs: owner occupier
To buy: £46 950
To rent: £42 per week

A number of changes are taking place in MEDC inner city areas:
- Much of the housing has been removed and replaced by either high-rise flats or modern terraces. Recent changes have improved living conditions and services in these areas.
- Many people have been moved to flats in other parts of the city.
- Inner city factories are difficult to reach on busy and narrow roads and many have relocated to the edge of the city.
- In recent years, rather than knocking down old houses many of them have been modernised. This is called gentrification.

Action Point

Use figure 3.9. Rank the housing types according to their nearness to the CBD and according their cost to buy. To what extent is it true that housing improves as you move away from the city centre?

Action Point

Look at map J in the colour resources section, which shows the City Challenge area, taken from the 1997 Progress Report. List four improvements that have been made.

Changing the inner city: who makes the decisions?

You have seen in the study of Sanjay Gandhi Nagar that different people and groups of people can influence the decision-making process. Changes in the Westcotes and Castle wards of Leicester took place as the result of the City Challenge Scheme that was introduced by the government in 1991. Local councils were asked to bid for money to use for improvements to inner city areas.

What changes were made?

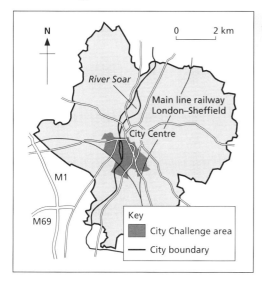

◀ **3.10** *The City Challenge scheme*

Who made the decisions? The Leicester City Challenge Board (LCCB) was set up as a partnership between different groups of people who had an interest in improving the City Challenge area.

Targets set in 1993 for 1998
Create 2065 new jobs
Build or improve 1425 homes
Start 130 new businesses
Reduce crime
Reclaim derelict land and create green spaces
Develop community projects

Outcomes in 1998
Almost 3000 jobs created
Over 4500 houses built or improved
Over 250 businesses set up
Street lighting increased; free locks and security advice provided
Five pocket parks plus a two hectare park created
Projects include childcare for working parents, lunchtime clubs for elderly Asians

Central government money
↓
LCCB
↓

Chief Executive	Public Sector	Private Sector	Community
	Leicestershire Health Authority	Training and Enterprise Council	Tenants' associations
	Leicester City Council	Chamber of Commerce	Residents' associations
	Leicestershire County Council	Asian business groups	Disabled groups
		Leicester University	Religious groups
		De Montfort University	
		Business Council representative	

Hints and Tips!

Don't forget that most locations may be described by giving the distance and direction from a known place.

When asked to justify a decision about service provision, your explanation should include an understanding of what people may need and also what is already provided in the area.

Action Point

Look at map J in the colour resources section. There are two areas of derelict land. Describe their locations. Leisure services are being built on one of these areas. Suggest one group of people who will benefit from these. Explain your choice. What would you do with the other area of derelict land? Justify your decision.

Action Point

To what extent has the development plan been a success? Use evidence from figure 3.10 to support your answer.

The Westcotes and Castle ward change is an example of urban renewal. The main structure of the area remains the same and it is modernised to take into account the needs of people living there. Some inner city areas have been subjected to comprehensive development by knocking down the existing buildings and starting again. This mainly happened in the United Kingdom during the 1960s. Old terraced housing disappeared and new dwellings, often multi-storey flats, took their place. There are advantages and disadvantages of comprehensive redevelopment like this.

Advantages	Disadvantages
New places for people to live	Communities ripped apart
Building high creates more green space	High-rise flats reduce privacy
People and traffic are separated	High-rise danger for children
Creates space for new retail parks	Flats encourage crime

Many of the new developments of the 1960s have already been knocked down. Others have been or are being renewed.

Providing services in the city

It is difficult to make simple statements about services because they are so varied: shops, somewhere to play, a place to sit down and be entertained, emergency services like police, fire and ambulance. These are all important to people either throughout their lives or at particular times. You will be able to think of others.

Some people find it difficult to reach the services they want or need. Others find it relatively easy. It is this accessibility to services that is so important to our quality of life.

▼ *3.11* City services

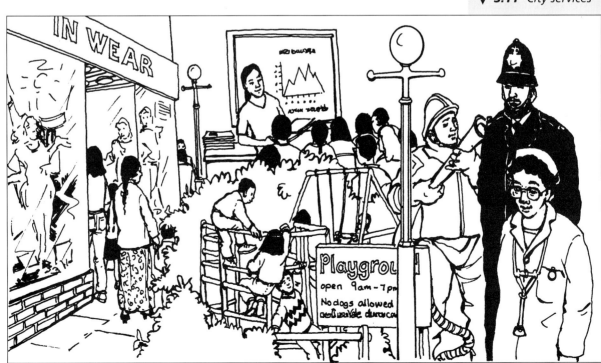

Action Point

Explain the difference between the public and private sectors. Suggest which groups will have the least and the most power in the LCCB. Explain your choices. Why is it important to include the views of people living in the area?

Action Point

Write a 'So what?' statement for each of these advantages and disadvantages. For example, 'Communities ripped apart means that people may be separated from their neighbours.'

▼ *3.12 Factors affecting access to services*

The distribution of one service in a city: shops

A service on which we all depend is shops. The distribution of shops within a town or city is the result of the way in which the urban area has grown and developed.

The Central Business District, for example, is in the middle of a city. It is, therefore, the centre of communications and so large numbers of people find it easy to access. This attracts many shops and other services.

On the edge of cities, often near motorway junctions, are recently built out-of-town shopping centres. These use the cheaper land on the city's edge and mainly attract car travellers, although many have regular bus services.

The map below is a transect from the centre of Leicester to its south-western suburbs. Although all urban areas are different, the pattern of shops is similar to that found in most towns and cities in the UK.

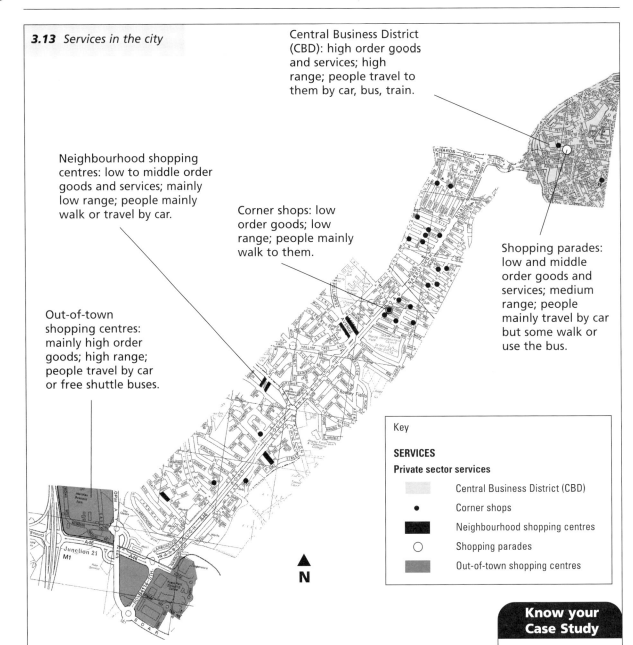

3.13 *Services in the city*

Central Business District (CBD): high order goods and services; high range; people travel to them by car, bus, train.

Neighbourhood shopping centres: low to middle order goods and services; mainly low range; people mainly walk or travel by car.

Corner shops: low order goods; low range; people mainly walk to them.

Shopping parades: low and middle order goods and services; medium range; people mainly travel by car but some walk or use the bus.

Out-of-town shopping centres: mainly high order goods; high range; people travel by car or free shuttle buses.

Key

SERVICES

Private sector services

	Central Business District (CBD)
•	Corner shops
▬	Neighbourhood shopping centres
○	Shopping parades
▨	Out-of-town shopping centres

N

You need to know some important terms:

- **The order of goods:** low order goods cost little and people buy them often – they are also called convenience goods. High order goods are expensive and people buy them infrequently – they are also called comparison goods.
- **The range:** this is about the distance people are prepared to travel to visit shops. People travel a long way to shops that have a high range and only a short distance to those that have a low range. The area from which people travel to a shop or shopping centre is called its catchment area.

Know your Case Study

Use the information on pages 53 and 54, or from another service you have studied to answer this Case Study question: 'For a service you have studied, describe its distribution and explain how it is accessible to different groups of people.'

Leaving the cities ... counter-urbanisation

In LEDCs the main trend is for people to migrate to urban areas and the percentage of people living in urban areas grows each year. You should already have revised the reasons for and effects of these movements.

Many MEDCs are showing the opposite trend. People are leaving the urban areas and moving to the countryside to live. Reasons for such migration can be seen as push and pull factors.

As well as these factors, a major reason for the move to the countryside has been ownership of motor vehicles. It is now possible to live in a village and commute to the city daily in order to work. Many villages on the edges of cities have changed their character from being traditional farming villages to becoming commuter settlements.

▲ *3.14 The push of the city*

▲ *3.15 The pull of the countryside*

1 Atmospheric pollution
2 Congested roads
3 Fear of crime

4 Clean air
5 Empty roads
6 Friendly community

The effect on rural communities

Slow changes have always taken place in rural communities. The recent movement of commuters into some villages has been rapid and has had a major impact on the people who have lived in the village for a long time.

1 Villages have grown physically

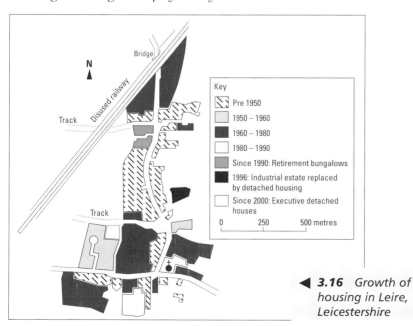

Key

Pre 1950
1950 – 1960
1960 – 1980
1980 – 1990
Since 1990: Retirement bungalows
1996: Industrial estate replaced by detached housing
Since 2000: Executive detached houses

0   250   500 metres

Bridge
Disused railway
Track
Track
N

◀ *3.16 Growth of housing in Leire, Leicestershire*

Hints and Tips!

When being asked to describe distribution as part of a Case Study, it may be useful to show the distribution by drawing a carefully labelled sketch map.

Action Point

Link the following 'so what?' statements to the push or pull factors above:
(a) so there is little risk of lung disease and a healthier lifestyle.
(b) so people are afraid to go out at night and feel insecure.
(c) so the journey to work is slow and accident rates are high.
(d) so there is a feeling of being secure and needed.
(e) so travel is easy and safe.
(f) so there is a high incidence of lung disease and an unhealthy population.

Action Point

Look at the map 3.16. Describe the location of the pre-1950 village. Describe how the village has grown since 1950. Suggest two ways in which the growth of the village may have affected people living in the pre-1950 houses.

2 *Village services have changed*

As villages have become commuter settlements, there has been a great impact on village services. The new villagers usually work outside the community, they often have access to more than one car per family, they own the house in which they live, and they have a high disposable income.

Figure 3.17 shows changes in services in the village of Leire. Some services have closed down.

It is not just a story of closed services. There are a number of recently opened services in Leire. Although some of them, like having mains gas supplied to the house, benefit all members of the community, others benefit different groups of people.

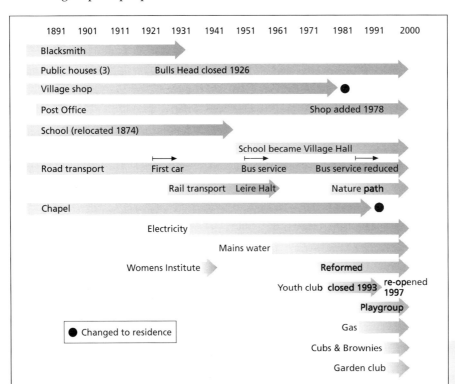

3.17 *Changing services, 1891–2000*

Action Point

Use figure 3.17 to list those services that have closed or been reduced in Leire since 1961. For one of these closed services suggest why it closed. How might a future closure of the bus service affect different groups of people in the village?

Action Point

Explain how the new villagers may affect village services.

Action Point

For each of the following groups of people name one recently opened service from which they will benefit. Explain how they will benefit:

- Old age pensioner

- Teenager

- Couple with young child

Exam practice

(a) Describe the housing in the foreground of photograph 3.7 on page 47. (3 marks)

(b) How is the housing in the background different from that in the foreground? (4 marks)

(c) Which housing offers the best opportunities for a high quality of life? Explain your choice. (4 marks)

Countryside conflict

People have more leisure time than was previously the case. They also have more money and transport to enable them to use this leisure time in areas away from their homes. Many urban dwellers visit rural areas of natural beauty. Quite unintentionally, they are damaging those environments that they wish to see.

Places that attract very large numbers of tourists are called *honeypot* sites.

The effects of too many tourists on honeypot sites are quite varied. Some of the most damaging effects are those that destroy the landform itself.

Action Point

Look at map F and photo G in the colour resources section. Describe the location of Stickle Tarn. What evidence is there that Stickle Tarn attracts many visitors? Give two reasons why Stickle Tarn attracts many visitors.

◀ *3.18 Footpath in Stickle Ghyll, 1970s*

It is possible to tackle the damage to honeypot sites in three major ways:

1   Restriction of activities. Within England and Wales there are a number of National Parks. They have been set up in order to protect the environment from the damaging effects of the activities of people. They restrict the activities of local people by strictly controlling the numbers of new buildings and insisting on the use of traditional building activities. They also restrict the activities of visitors by, for example, not allowing motorised boats on many lakes or by keeping certain valleys clear of tourists' cars.
2   Creating counter-attractions. Create other attractions in the area to take pressure off the sites most under stress.
3   Repairing the damage done by the visitors.

Action Point

Describe the scene in photo 3.18. Explain how Stickle Tarn being a honeypot site has affected the Stickle Ghyll footpath.

Hints and Tips!

When asked to *describe* what you see in a photo, do just that. Do *not* explain how it got that way.

◀ *3.19 Other effects of tourists on the environment and people*

A problem-solving activity

At the end of your course you will be expected to sit a problem-solving paper. In its early part you will be asked questions about the unit of work on which the paper is set. You will then be introduced to an area and its geography. By the end of the paper you will be expected to make a *justified* decision about some aspect of how the area is to be managed for the future.

You have now been led through a number of questions that have introduced you to the Langdale Valley. You have been shown how people's activities have affected the landforms found in the valley. You have also been shown how people can manage these activities.

In what follows you are being asked to show a plan for the future use of the Langdale valley. This is your brief:

Any future use of the Langdale Valley should meet the needs of the following groups of people:

1   Local people in an area where unemployment is high and there are few work opportunities outside of tourism. Most tourist jobs are seasonal in nature.

2   Environmentalists – any future plans should recognise the fragile nature of the environment and the need to conserve it for future generations.

3   Visitors who wish to take part in activities without feeling restricted by rules and regulations.

Action Point

Compare the scene in 3.18 with photo H in the colour resources section.

Use this information and Table I in the colour resources section to describe how the needs of both the environment and the visitors have been met by the work that has been done. Is this an example of item 1, 2 or 3 in the list on this page? Explain your choice.

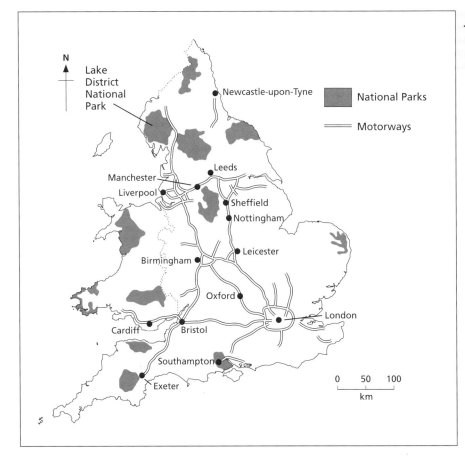

◀ *3.20 The location of National Parks in England and Wales*

Hints and Tips!

When asked for map evidence make sure that you do quote evidence from the map. When using an OS map include grid references.

Hints and Tips!

Sketch 3.19 and map 3.20 provide information you may wish to use in your answer to the problem-solving activity above.

Suggestions have been made as to how the valley should be managed in future:

There is high unemployment in this area. Apart from farming there is only tourism and that is mainly in the summer. Most jobs are seasonal. We have to encourage people to visit us throughout the year.

The environment in this area is beautiful. In places, though, it has been spoilt by too many visitors. We must encourage people to take part in activities that are less damaging to the environment and that spread the visitors across a wider area.

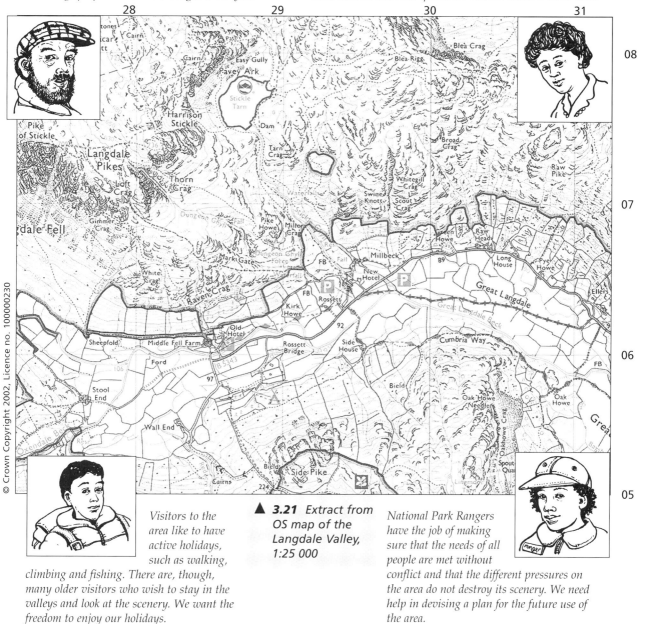

© Crown Copyright 2002, Licence no. 100000230

Visitors to the area like to have active holidays, such as walking, climbing and fishing. There are, though, many older visitors who wish to stay in the valleys and look at the scenery. We want the freedom to enjoy our holidays.

▲ *3.21 Extract from OS map of the Langdale Valley, 1:25 000*

National Park Rangers have the job of making sure that the needs of all people are met without conflict and that the different pressures on the area do not destroy its scenery. We need help in devising a plan for the future use of the area.

! Action Point

Draw and label your ideas on a copy of map 3.21, then write a letter to the Lake District Park Planning Board to explain and justify what you have done. Refer to map evidence in your explanation.

Terms and meanings: People and place

Here are some important terms for you to match up and learn. Try to match them up yourself before looking at the answers at the back of the book.

Term

Meaning

1 Census data

2 Central Business District (CBD)

3 Commuters

4 Comprehensive redevelopment

5 Council housing

6 Counter-urbanisation

7 Disposable income

8 Housing tenure

9 Inner city

10 Mega-cities

11 Migrants

12 Neighbourhood

13 National Parks

14 Non-government organisations

15 Receiving areas

16 Services

17 Source areas

18 Squatter settlements

19 Suburbs

20 Urbanisation

21 Urban dereliction

22 Urban renewal

23 Urban–rural fringe

A Cities having a population of over 10 million.

B People who live some distance from their place of work and who travel daily to and from work.

C The areas on the very edge of an urban area where it meets the countryside.

D Groups of people that work with communities in order to improve their quality of life. They are separated from official local and national government agencies but sometimes work with them.

E Those places that people leave when they migrate.

F The conditions under which a household inhabits its home. Common forms of housing tenure include owner-occupied, privately rented and council-rented.

G The process by which an increasing number of people live in towns and cities as opposed to the countryside. This could be the result of natural increase and/or migration.

H The area surrounding a person's home and containing many of the services important to that person. It has definite boundaries.

I The area found towards the edge of the city. In MEDCs they usually have low-density housing.

J Those places that people move to when they migrate.

K A type of housing tenure in which the houses are owned by local government and rented to the people who live in them.

L The zone surrounding the CBD in a city.

M The process by which derelict areas of a town or city are improved by upgrading existing buildings. This process is sometimes known as gentrification.

N In the middle of a town or city, this is its main commercial and shopping area.

O The neglect and decay of parts of a town or city.

P Features of an area that help improve the quality of life of people living in it. They range from shops to healthcare, entertainment and the provision of reliable supplies of clean water.

Q A housing policy in which areas of low-quality buildings are cleared and replaced by a new, higher-quality, living environment.

R Often illegal groupings of houses on the edges of LEDC cities built by the people who live in them from any materials they can find.

S The amount of money left when essential bills have been paid.

T The process by which people within a country live in the countryside as opposed to towns and cities. This could be by natural increase or migration.

U The information gained from an official population count – usually once every ten years.

V People who move from one place to another in order to live.

W Areas of outstanding natural beauty where there are strict controls on development to conserve wildlife and manage the interests of different

Unit 4: People, work and development

How and why do employment structures differ?

Everybody's labour may be classified as work. It is only called employment when people are paid for their labour. You are working now but not being paid!

Employment is divided into three broad areas:

- Primary – the growing or extraction of raw materials. Examples include fishing, forestry, agriculture, mining and quarrying.

- Secondary – the manufacturing and processing of goods. Examples include making goods in factories or assembly industries like car making.

- Tertiary – providing a service. Examples include medical and education services and the selling of goods in shops.

▼ **4.1** *Primary, secondary and tertiary*

The Brandt Report of 1980 divided the world into two halves. It did so to encourage the closing of the divide between economically rich and poor countries. Countries to the north side of the Brandt Line are said to be More Economically Developed Countries (MEDCs) and those on the south side of it are said to be Less Economically Developed Countries (LEDCs). Although countries have developed at different rates since that time and some people think the Brandt Line is out of date, this division is still used by many people.

The Brandt Line only reflects economic development. It ignores the fact that many countries or regions have developed complex social and cultural structures that are not accompanied by economic wealth as we understand it.

We continue, though, to use the terms LEDC and MEDC. One way of telling whether a country is an LEDC or an MEDC is by looking at its employment structure.

An LEDC is likely to have:
- a high percentage in *primary employment*. Many people will live in rural areas and subsistence farming will employ many of these. Little machinery will mean that almost all work is done by hand. Mineral resources are extracted in LEDCs often for processing in MEDCs.
- a low percentage in *secondary employment*. The country has little capital for investment in manufacturing and many goods are imported. Trans-national companies and the World Bank may have developed factories but much manufacturing is small-scale and often combined with farming.
- a fairly low percentage in *tertiary employment*. In order to afford services the country must create wealth. Services are paid for either directly by the user or indirectly through taxes. A country needs a high Gross Domestic Product (GDP) in order to be able to afford a large percentage of tertiary workers.

Action Point

What does having a high percentage of workers in primary industry suggest about a country? Describe the position of the Brandt Line on Map 4.2 on page 62. To what extent is the Brandt Line an accurate divide between MEDCs and LEDCs?

Hints and Tips!

When you are asked to give a definition, do *not* use the word you are asked to define as a part of your own definition.

Only give an example when asked to do so.

Do *not* give an example instead of a definition.

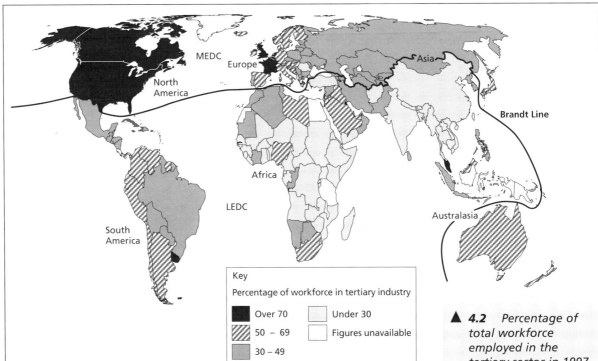

Key

Percentage of workforce in tertiary industry

■	Over 70	▨	Under 30
▨	50 – 69	□	Figures unavailable
▦	30 – 49		

▲ *4.2 Percentage of total workforce employed in the tertiary sector in 1997. The percentage employed in these service industries is taken as an indicator of economic development.*

An MEDC will have:

- a low percentage in *primary employment*. Since the Second World War farming and extractive industry have become heavily mechanised and fewer people are needed on the land.
- a higher percentage in *secondary industry*. This is often important in creating the country's wealth but percentages are not huge because much of the work is highly mechanised.
- a very high percentage in *tertiary industry*. These countries create the wealth needed for well-developed health and education services. Individual people living in the countries can afford to buy more goods and services like insurance. Banks and insurance companies in MEDCs attract business from overseas.

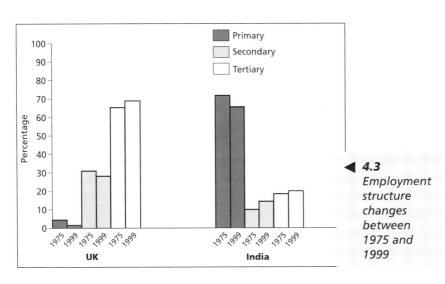

◄ *4.3 Employment structure changes between 1975 and 1999*

Action Point

Look at graph 4.3. Describe how the employment structure of the UK changed between 1975 and 1999. Compare these changes with those for India. Give three reasons for India's employment structure in 1999.

Hints and Tips!

Know your terms.

What is GDP?

Check out the important terms on page 74.

How do we measure well-being?

The main measures of well-being in a country are those that show how a country uses its wealth. A rich country (one with a high Gross Domestic Product (GDP)) will offer a higher standard of living to its population than a poor country (one with a low GDP). These, though, are averages and in all countries there is the whole range of people from very rich to very poor. Some services are provided by the 'State' but others must be paid for privately. People will, therefore, have a greater or lesser access to the range of services offered in that country according to their wealth.

Indicators of *standard of living* can include access to services:
- public spending on health (as percentage of GDP): India 1.3%; UK 6.6%
- adult literacy (percentage of adults who can read and write): India 51%; UK 99%.

Or could include the ability to buy goods:
- televisions per 100 people: India 6; UK 45.

Or could be a prediction:
- life expectancy at birth (in years): India 61.3; UK 76.7.

All of these depend upon the country's wealth:
- GDP per person: India $1 348; UK $ 18 340.

Quality of life is different from standard of living and is much more difficult to measure. In fact quality of life may include a person's standard of living but it might also include such things as the influence of family life, friendship, and whether or not a person is happy.

How do employment opportunities differ?

Employment opportunities are different from place to place and also in the same place at different times.

For example, it is said that there are differences between the UK regions. Since the Second World War there has been a decline in the traditional secondary industries found in the North and an increasing interest in the South East because of the importance of the London market for goods and its nearness to transport links to Europe. The pattern of unemployment is shifting all the time, though.

Similar differences may be seen in other countries. There is, for example, a contrast between the rich north and poor south in Italy.

Traditional industries include coal mining, iron and steelmaking, heavy engineering (like shipbuilding) and textiles. The reason they were located where they were was because coal was the main fuel used in manufacturing and it was expensive to transport.

Although reasons for the decline of individual industries are all slightly different, there are a number of general ones:
(a) a world-wide decline or drop in demand for the product, e.g. ships (*So what?*)
(b) the raw material once found in the area may have run out, e.g. coal, iron ore (*So what?*)
(c) competition from newly established industry abroad, especially countries that had been in the old British Empire and began processing their own raw materials rather than allowing them to come to the UK, e.g. textiles (*So what?*).

Action Point

List two ways in which India's standard of living is different from the UK's. Explain why each difference exists. Explain why the UK may be regarded as a more economically developed country than India.

Action Point

Match the following elaborations with statements (a) to (e) below and on the following page:

1 This has reduced demand for these older materials, creating job losses.

2 Means that primary producers have to look elsewhere for supplies.

3 Because labour is cheaper here, goods imported from these countries are cheaper and have put some UK manufacturers out of business.

4 Fewer sales world-wide means greater competition between the suppliers, and the closure of some workplaces.

5 More machinery and computerised systems are used in factories.

(d) competition from newer products or fuels that have replaced them, e.g. oil replacing coal, and plastics replacing many steel products (*So what?*)

(e) it is not always a decline in the industry that causes job losses and a decline in employment (*So what?*).

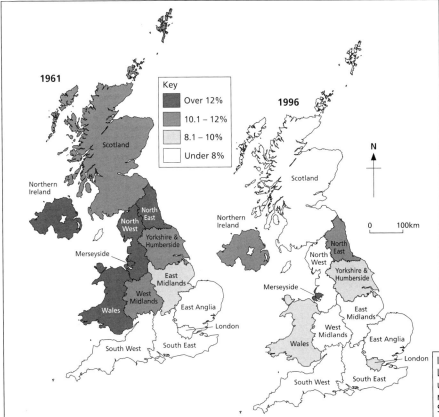

Action Point

Look at map 4.4 for 1961. Describe the distribution of areas of high unemployment.

◀ **4.4** *Percentage unemployed by UK Standard Regions*

In 1999, the North East (10.1%) and London (7.6%) had the highest unemployment rates. All other regions were below 7%, with the South East being the lowest at 3.6%.

Action Point

Describe the activity in photo 4.5. Suggest how this work is done now. Add a 'So what' statement to explain how it may have affected employment opportunities.

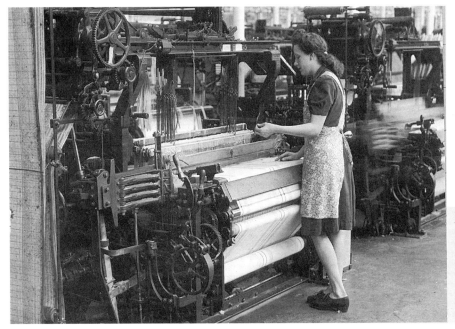

◀ **4.5** *Working in a Lancashire cotton mill. Many traditional jobs like these were lost in the 1950s and 1960s, with disastrous effects on people's lives*

The effects of industrial decline

Whatever the reason for a decline in employment opportunities, the job losses have an effect on the individual and on the area.

On the individual it could result in redundancy or part-time work.

◀ **4.6** *Positive:*
- *creates more leisure time*
- *allows more time with family*

◀ **4.7** *Negative:*
- *reduces income*
- *results in low self-esteem*
- *loss of house and other property*
- *reduces standard of living*
- *causes family arguments*

1 closure
2 many people out of work
3 people in related or support industries are made redundant
4 less money spent on services and goods
5 people made redundant in shops and services
6 less money in area
7 even less money in area
8 area becomes run down and often vandalised
9 shops and services close down
10 it's difficult to attract new industry

◀ **4.8** *The negative multiplier*

Action Point

Look at spiral 4.8. Describe how the closure of a steelworks may affect individual workers and communities.

Hints and Tips!

When a question asks for a response that touches on two different groups, you will not gain full marks if you only write about one. In this case you must write about the effects on both individuals *and* communities.

If only a few people in an area are made redundant, the effects on the individual person may be great but those on the area are relatively small. The effects on an area as the result of the closure of an industry that was a major employer is completely different. This causes a large percentage of the area's workers to be made redundant. Examples may include the closure of a steelworks or a coalmine.

The effects on an area of such closures are called the *negative multiplier*.

Turning it all around

Often areas do not improve until Government has stepped in and put money into the area. The two main sources of finance for areas in decline in the UK are national government and the European Union.

Wherever the money comes from it can be used to help attract new firms to set up in the area. These firms are often *multi-national companies* (MNCs). They are also called *trans-national corporations* (TNCs): companies that have their head office in one country, usually an MEDC, and factories in several others.

The reasons for setting up are often quite complex but there are some general points that apply to most MNCs that have set up in the UK:
- By manufacturing in the EU they avoid trade barriers.
- UK wages are low compared with many other EU countries.
- There are few strikes in the UK.
- English is either the first or second language in many countries.

▼ **4.9**   *LG's global presence*

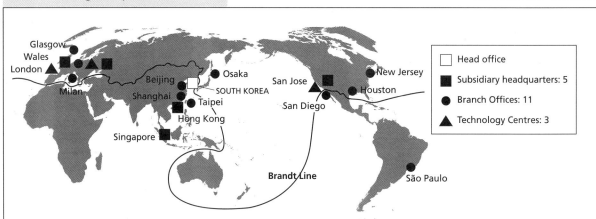

The choice to locate in a region within the UK is often the result of the package of incentives that is offered, such as development grants and low taxes. Areas that receive extra help in putting together incentive packages are called 'Assisted Areas'.

One MNC that has set up in the UK is LG (formerly known as Lucky Goldstar).

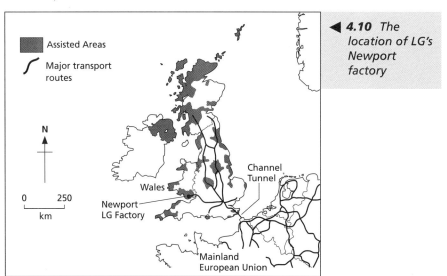

◀ **4.10** *The location of LG's Newport factory*

Action Point

Look at map 4.9. In which country is LG's head office? Describe the distribution of its branch offices.

Action Point

Use map 4.10 to give three reasons why LG chose Newport.

Action Point

Use map K in the colour resources section to describe the location of the LG factory. Use map evidence to give two reasons why it was built here.

Label a sketch of photo L in the colour resources section to show the factory buildings, car park space and room for expansion. Suggest how the building of the factory may have affected the environment.

The effects of industrial growth

When a major employer sets up in an area it has a *positive multiplier* effect.

One element of both the positive and the negative multipliers is the way in which industries are often attracted to each other. Coal used as a source of fuel caused a huge number of firms to locate on the coalfields. When this ran out or was replaced by forms of power that allowed people to locate almost anywhere (e.g. electricity), the industry moved away. Steelmaking would attract those industries that use steel as a raw material.

Hints and Tips!

When asked for map evidence make sure that you do quote evidence from the map. When using an OS map include grid references.

4.11 The positive multiplier

9 new jobs created

10 industrial development

8 jobs created in related or support industries

6 more money spent on services and goods

7 more money in area

5 new jobs created in shops and services

3 more shops and services open

4 even more money in improving the area

2 more taxes to spend on improving the area

1 new industry is attracted

Action Point

Draw a copy of the positive multiplier spiral. Use information from 4.12 to add detail of how the new LG factory should affect the Newport area.

It is not only jobs that *directly* rely on the industry that are affected. A new industry can also create *indirect* employment opportunities.

'The building of the factories has already provided jobs in construction. Most seeking jobs at LG will live within a reasonable travel-to-work radius of Newport but companies elsewhere can also benefit from LG. The two factories, employing over 6 000 people, will need materials from production-line robotics to toilet paper, and services from banking to window cleaning. We estimate there will be around 15 000 extra supplier and component jobs. Already 40 potential suppliers – 26 of them in Wales – have been visited by LG personnel.'

◄ **4.12** Welsh Development Agency

Action Point

Explain how the changes reported in 4.13 might affect employment in the Newport area.

APRIL 1998 – LG REVIEWS £1.7 BILLION INVESTMENT IN WALES

Although it is employing 2500 workers at its electronics factory near Newport, the LG company has decided not to open the LG Semicon plant due to the financial crisis in South Korea. The empty building has been sold to Hyundai, another South Korean multi-national. When the new owners have developed a new microchip it intends to open the factory. However, the financial situation must be stable first ...'

◄ **4.13** Change may be rapid

The work on the last few pages should have shown that employment opportunities are always changing.

The wider picture

We have already seen that in LEDCs there is a high percentage of workers in primary industry and that much of the work in both the primary and the secondary sectors is done by hand with little use of machinery.

Some LEDCs are developing rapidly and even in those that are not there are often areas in which highly automated industry has been developed. Countries that are recognised as having been LEDCs and that have developed their economies and manufacturing industry quickly are known as newly industrialised countries (NICs).

In some of these cases the money for such development again comes from MNCs. They may be given incentives by the governments of individual countries. It is also possible that investment has come from agencies like the World Bank and the International Monetary Fund (IMF), organisations set up by MEDCs to help LEDCs to develop. Here the money is loaned at special low interest rates.

Whatever the reason for their development, such new industries have benefits to the company and effects on the country.

Benefits to the company often include:
- cheap land
- purpose-built facilities
- low tax and rent rates
- a cheap, hard-working labour force.

Effects on the country could be both positive and negative.

Positive:
- a movement of high-tech industry into the country
- the development of a skilled labour force
- the attraction of more industry to the area
- greater exports bringing in more money
- improved world status.

Negative:
- creation of a great divide between 'haves' and 'have-nots' in society
- environmental destruction and noise and atmospheric pollution
- a foreign company may close the works without warning.

Action Point

Look back at maps 4.4 on page 64. How did the distribution of UK unemployment change between 1961 and 1996?

Hints and Tips!

Although the word is not used, you are asked to *compare* 1961 and 1996. Make sure you use words like 'but' and 'whereas'.

Know your Case Study

For an area where job opportunities have changed: name the area; describe how the job opportunities have changed; explain how these changes have affected people (this task is a Case Study and worth 5 marks on the Foundation Tier paper and 8 marks on the Higher Tier). Use either the information for India on page 69, or another Case Study from your revision notes. Mark your work according to the Foundation or Higher Tier mark scheme on page 13.

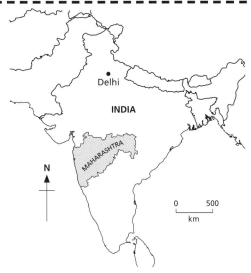

IT in India

The Government Leads:

- National IT Task Force set up in May 1998.

- Followed by State Governments setting up their own Task Forces.

- Most of India's States now have their own Departments of Information Technology.

- The Government encourages IT companies to set up by giving tax concessions, including 100% income tax exemption on exported services that use IT, and no duty is charged on the import of IT-related raw materials and components.

Action at the State level: Maharashtra State:

- Mumbai provides a 'state of the art' infrastructure for IT industry, including Infotech Parks.

- Software Technology Parks have been developed at Pune and Nagpur.

- A Hardware Park is being set up near Mumbai.

- There is an Institute of Information Technology at Mumbai and several engineering colleges are already operating.

- The State Government offices are being computerised.

- Maharashtra State has begun a 'Wired Villages' project aimed at using ICT to improve communications in rural areas.

Benefits:

- The incentives have attracted IT MNCs from the USA, Europe and Japan.

- Software exports are rising rapidly.

- Many service industries using IT now use India as a base. These include airlines, banks and health agencies.

- Increased employment is available for Indian people in the IT manufacturing and service areas.

Action Point

(a) Use information in 4.14 to describe how governments are introducing IT to India.

(b) Use information on pages 68–69 to explain how this will affect the country and its people.

◀ **4.14** *IT in India*

Hints and Tips!

When asked for the effects on a country and its people:

- look at both the country and its economy, and at individuals or groups of people

- look at both the positive and negative effects.

The world of trade

Countries survive by trading with one another. No country produces all the goods it requires for its people and all countries must import some items. Likewise, all countries produce more of some products than are needed for its own people; these materials are exported.

Traditionally LEDCs have been exporters of the products of primary industry like agricultural produce and minerals. MEDCs have been importers of these materials and exporters of manufactured goods.

While all trade is between individual countries, some countries have come together to form trading groups. These may be the result of:
- historical factors, e.g. the Newly Independent States were all members of the former USSR
- being geographically close together, e.g. the European Union
- being major producers of a particular product, e.g. OPEC members are all mineral oil exporting countries.

Advantages of being a member of a trading group include:
- being able to control the price of common exports
- access to a large market with no tariffs imposed on your goods
- protection from produce of countries outside the trading group by the use of tariffs and quotas on the goods of outsiders.

In spite of this, the rules of trade seem to favour MNCs and MEDCs. The LEDC countries seem to receive very little of the true value of their produce. This is now being challenged by some organisations, for example the Fairtrade group.

Hints and Tips!

In a question that asks you to describe the effects of a change in job or work opportunities, make sure that you adapt the multiplier effect (either positive or negative) to meet the needs of your answer.

Action Point

Describe the distribution of countries in the European Union. Compare this with the distribution of OPEC countries. Suggest two reasons for the differences you have described.

▼ **4.15** *Some trading groups*

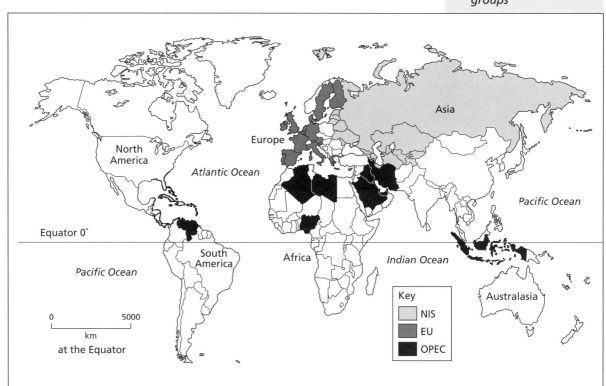

FAIRTRADE BANANAS
Guarantees a **better deal** for Third World Producers
Fairtrade
Windward Island banana farmers who are part of the Windward certified grower scheme receive a fair price for their labou
DO NOT REFRIGERATE

The Fairtrade mark goes on foods produced by independent growers and farmers in LEDCs. They cost a little extra to ensure that producers earn enough to look after their families. A Fairtrade label means the workers get:
• recognised trade unions
• no child labour
• decent working conditions
• a price that covers production
• an extra cost to improve conditions.

◀ **4.16** Challenging traditional trade structures

Is aid the answer?

Involvement of the World Bank and the International Monetary Fund (IMF) has usually been to provide the money to create large development projects. While these often provide advantages for some people in the country, they create few jobs and the majority of the people remain poor. For many countries, repayment of the loans may prove very difficult.

Aid takes three forms:
- *Bilateral aid* is given by the government of one country to the government of another.
- *Multilateral aid* is given by governments to international organisations like the United Nations Children's Fund (UNICEF).
- *Non-government organisation (NGO) aid* is from groups like charities and religious organisations to countries and groups in need of help.

Aid may be applied in one of two ways:
- As an emergency reaction to a major problem or disaster.
- As a strategy to enable people to take greater control of their own lives.

Although the first is necessary in the event of such disasters as flooding and droughts, most aid agencies aim at the second, more sustainable, approach.

Opinions differ as to whether large or small scale improvements are the most appropriate route to development.

Large-scale improvements (like huge dams):
- are very expensive
- are environmentally unfriendly
- are few in number
- reach a small percentage of the population.

Most small-scale projects use intermediate technology, like the *Village Platform*. Any improvements are small, cheap to operate, easy to repair and enable the people receiving the aid to develop their skills and become more self-sufficient.

Small-scale improvements:
- are relatively cheap
- may be made in almost all villages
- reach a large percentage of the population.

Action Point

Explain how Fairtrade might affect an LEDC worker.

Suggest its effects on MEDC consumers.

Action Point

What might be the main advantages of being a member of (a) the NIS, and (b) OPEC?

Action Point

Look at photo N in the colour resources section. Describe the main features of the Village Platform. Explain how the Village Platform may improve the quality of life of the villagers who use it. Suggest any difficulties it may create.

The price to pay

All developments have an effect on the environment and on people. The main effects can be summarised as:

- Atmospheric pollution including global warming, international acid rain and the local effects on habitats of fumes from factories and road vehicles.
- Visual and noise pollution suffered by both people and wildlife living near factories, mines and quarries.
- Water polluted by its use for dumping toxic waste, the washing of fertiliser into rivers from farmland and the use of water for cooling thermal power stations.
- Land scarred by quarrying and containing the waste heaps of mining operations.

In fact, every time an area is developed there is a negative effect on the environment.

A fresh start?

In many old industrial areas the traditional industries have declined. Many coalmines and steelworks have closed down. They have left behind, though, landscapes of industrial dereliction. The visual impact is one that reduces the quality of life of people living in these areas, and many of the sites are dangerous.

National and regional governments in some areas have put a great deal of effort into repairing the damage caused by previous generations.

The Emscher Landscape Park

During the nineteenth century the Ruhr area of Germany developed as an important industrial centre. The expansion of mining, steelmaking and heavy engineering caused great environmental damage. During the Second World War the area was heavily damaged by bombing and since then traditional industries have died out. A severely damaged landscape was left.

The Association of Ruhr District Local Authorities and seventeen towns in the Emscher Valley linked together to create a programme intended to repair their industrial damage. Two-thirds of the money came from Government 'State Aid' programmes and the rest from private investment.

Improvements have been made in five areas:
1 Creating an Emscher Landscape Park: this includes projects of different scales ranging from the redevelopment of large areas of land to the planting of small areas of trees.
2 The regeneration of the Emscher river system: redesigning water courses and constructing new sewage treatment plants.
3 Creating new work in this area of high unemployment: putting in commercial, service industry and science parks. They are all built on former industrial sites.
4 Building new houses on derelict land and the renewal of many more that had sound structures but were out of date inside.
5 Converting old industrial buildings to new uses, like the inside of a gasometer as an exhibition hall.

These changes are aimed not only at improving the environment but also allow for the sustainable development of the area by creating new job and housing opportunities and increased access to recreation.

Action Point

Look at photo O in the colour resources section. Describe how the development may have affected the environment and people.

Action Point

Use maps A–C in 4.17 on the next page to describe the location of the Emscher Landscape Park. Use photos O and P in the colour resources section to describe the damage being caused to the environment and ways it is being improved. Explain how these changes will affect local people.

Hints and Tips!

The study of the Emscher Landscape Park is another that you could use as a Case Study in preparation for your examination. Don't forget, though, that you have a number of Case Studies that you have completed during your GCSE course. Do you have one of your own that covers the same principles of industrial dereliction and improvement?

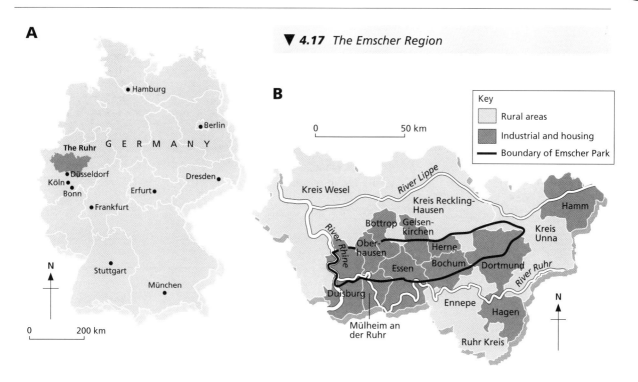

▼ 4.17 *The Emscher Region*

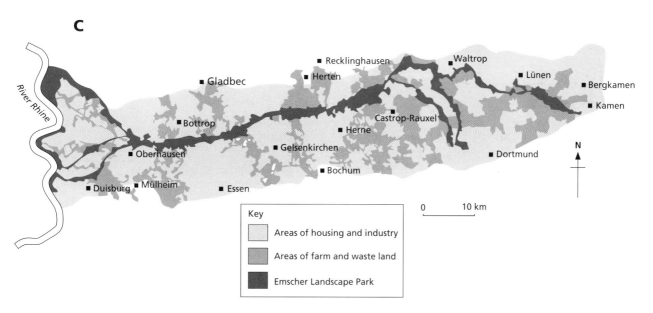

Exam practice

Case Study. An area where job opportunities have changed.
For a country or region where job opportunities have changed, name the country or region, describe how the job opportunities have changed and explain how these changes have affected people and the environment.

(a) Name the country or region.

(b) Describe how the job opportunities have changed.

(c) Explain how these changed have affected people and the environment.

Know your Case Study

Terms and meanings: People, work and development

Here are some important terms for you to match up and learn. The answers are at the back of the book. Use them only to help when you have tried to match them for yourself.

Meaning

Term

1 Common Agricultural Policy

2 Development agencies

3 Economic recession

4 Economic recovery

5 European Union

6 Gross Domestic Product

7 Independence

8 Informal employment

9 Infrastructure

10 Intermediate aid

11 Inward investment

12 Multi-national corporation (MNC)

13 Negative multiplier

14 Net exporters

15 Net importers

16 Newly industrialising country

17 Positive multiplier

18 Quality of life

19 Self-employed

20 Standard of living

21 Subsistence farming

22 Traditional aid

A Factors that affect a person's quality of life and which can be measured. Many such measures are to do with possessions.

B When a government takes on sole responsibility for making decisions about how to run a country.

C Help usually given by organisations in MEDCs to people living in LEDCs. It often involves small-scale, labour-intensive schemes aimed at providing a sustainable future.

D A period during which industrial activity rises from a period of economic recession, new jobs are created and the positive multiplier operates.

E The structure of communications and services required to support economic development in a particular area.

F The happiness, well-being and satisfaction of a person.

G Events that follow the decline of investment in a region such as decreased spending, the loss of jobs and out-migration.

H Created by the UK government to provide help as grants, loans, ready-built factories and infrastructure to attract investment into areas of decline and high unemployment.

I Where a person chooses to work for him/herself as a paid employee and accepts the responsibility of paying deductions such as taxes to the government.

J A country that may be classed as an LEDC but which is developing a large secondary industry sector.

K Help usually given by organisations in MEDCs to people living in LEDCs. It often involves lending large sums of money to develop large schemes such as dams.

L Countries or regions that sell a greater value of goods and services than they buy each year.

M A trading group of European countries formally set up in 1993 to follow on from the European Community (EC).

N Unofficial jobs that have no set hours or rates of pay. People who are employed in this way may avoid paying tax and are usually self-employed.

O A period of decline during which some industrial activity closes, people become unemployed and the negative multiplier operates.

P A form of agriculture where most of the produce meets the basic needs of the farmer's family with little for sale. It differs from commercial farming where most of the produce is grown for sale.

Q Investment into a country usually from multi-national companies (MNC) based in another country.

R Events that follow major investments in a region such as increased spending, the creation of other jobs and in-migration.

S A large company that has its head offices in one country (usually an MEDC) and factories in a number of other countries. They are also called trans-national companies.

T Countries or regions that buy a greater value of goods and services than they sell each year.

U The total value of all the goods and services produced in a country in one year by all the people living in that country.

V Strategies for the control and development of farming that have been adopted by all members of the European Union.

Case Study practice

Use the tables on the next pages to match your own Case Studies to questions that have appeared in recent examinations. For each Case Study, give its name and location and then *select* the information you would use to answer the *describe* and *explain* parts of each question.

Examination question	Name of Case Study	Location	Describe	Explain
▼ Climate, environment and people: Foundation Tier				
For an ecosystem you have studied: (i) Name the ecosystem. (ii) Describe the main features of the ecosystem. (iii) Explain how it is used by people.				
For a climate type you have studied: (i) Name the type of climate. (ii) Describe the type of climate. (iii) Explain how the climate affects the lives of people during the whole year.				
For a weather event you have studied: (i) Say what it was and where it happened. (ii) Describe how the weather event affected people. (iii) Explain why the weather event took place.				
For an ecosystem you have studied that is being damaged: (i) Name the ecosystem and state where it is located. (ii) Describe how the ecosystem is being damaged. (iii) Explain what is being done or could be done to reduce the damage.				
▼ Climate, environment and people: Higher Tier				
For an ecosystem you have studied: (i) Name the ecosystem. (ii) Describe the main features of the ecosystem. (iii) Explain how different groups of people have changed the ecosystem.				
For a climate type you have studied: (i) Name the type of climate. (ii) Describe the type of climate. (iii) Explain how it affects people and the environment over a whole year.				

Examination question	Name of Case Study	Location	Describe	Explain
▼ Climate, environment and people: Higher Tier continued				
For a weather event you have studied: (i) Name the weather event. (ii) Describe how the weather event affected different groups of people and the environment. (iii) Explain why the weather event took place.				
For an ecosystem you have studied that is being damaged: (i) Name and locate the ecosystem that is being damaged. (ii) Describe how the ecosystem is eing damaged. (iii) Explain how different groups of people or organisations are trying to conserve this ecosystem.				
▼ People and place: Foundation Tier				
For a planning scheme you have studied: (i) Name the place. (ii) Describe the planning scheme. (iii) Explain how the scheme affected the quality of housing for people.				
For a service you have studied: (i) Name the place and service. (ii) Describe the distribution of the service. (iii) Explain the distribution of the service.				
For a housing area in a town or city you have studied: (i) Name the town or city you have studied. (ii) Describe the housing area and groups of people who live in it. (iii) Explain why these groups live in the housing area.				
For an area you have studied that has been improved in an MEDC town or city: (i) Name the town or city and area that has been improved. (ii) Describe how the area has been improved (draw maps or diagrams if you wish). (iii) Explain how successful these improvements have been.				

Examination question	Name of Case Study	Location	Describe	Explain
▼ People and place: Higher Tier				
For a planning scheme you have studied: (i) Name the area. (ii) Describe the planning scheme. (iii) Explain how the scheme affected the quality of housing for different groups of people.				
For a service you have studied: (i) Name the place and service. (ii) Draw a sketch map to show the distribution of the service. (iii) Explain the distribution of the service.				
For a named town or city in an MEDC or an LEDC you have studied: (i) Name the town or city. (ii) Describe the distribution of different types of housing (draw diagrams or sketch maps if you wish). (iii) Explain why different groups of people live in these housing areas.				
For an area you have studied that has been improved in an MEDC town or city: (i) Name and locate the area. (ii) Describe the problems that needed solving in the area. (iii) Explain how successful the improvements have been for different groups of people living in or close to this area.				
▼ People, work and development: Foundation Tier				
For a country or region you have studied where overseas investment has taken place: (i) Name the country or region. (ii) Describe the job opportunities created. (iii) Explain other effects on the country or region.				
For a primary or secondary industrial development you have studied: (i) Name the industrial development. (ii) Describe its location. (iii) Explain why it is located there.				

Examination question	Name of Case Study	Location	Describe	Explain
▼ *People, work and development: Foundation Tier continued*				
For a country or region you have studied outside the UK where job opportunities have changed: (i) Name the country or region. (ii) Describe how the job opportunities have changed. (iii) Explain how these changes have affected people.				
For a primary or tertiary industry you have studied: (i) Name and locate the industry. (ii) Describe the activity. (iii) Explain how it has affected the environment.				
▼ *People, work and development: Higher Tier*				
For a named country or region you have studied: (i) Describe how overseas investment has affected employment opportunities. (ii) Explain any social and environmental impacts that the overseas investment has had on the country or region.				
For a primary or secondary industrial development you have studied: (i) Name the industrial development. (ii) Draw an annotated sketch map to show its location. (iii) Explain any advantages and disadvantages of its present location.				
For a country or region you have studied outside the UK where employment opportunities are changing: (i) Name the country or region. (ii) Describe how the employment opportunities are changing. (iii) Explain how these changes are affecting people and the area.				
For a primary or tertiary economic activity you have studied that has affected people and the environment: (i) Name the economic activity. (ii) Describe the location of the economic activity (iii) Explain how the economic activity has affected people and the environment.				

Examination question	Name of Case Study	Location	Describe	Explain
▼ Water, landforms and people: Foundation Tier				
(i) Name a water management scheme in an MEDC. (ii) Describe the scheme (use maps and diagrams if you wish). (iii) Explain how it has affected the lives of people.				
(i) Name and locate a river or coastal landform that has been formed by the sea or rivers. (ii) Describe the landform. (iii) Explain how it has been formed.				
(i) Name and locate a landform which is being managed by people. (ii) Describe the landform. (iii) Explain how it is being managed by people.				
(i) Name a place that has experienced a water shortage. (ii) Describe how the water shortage affected the lives of people. (iii) Explain what caused the water shortage.				
(i) Name and locate a coastal or river landform you have studied. (ii) Describe how it was formed (use maps and diagrams if you wish). (iii) Explain how it affects people living in the area.				
(i) Name an area where flooding has taken place. (ii) Describe how the flood affected people. (iii) Explain what is being done or could be done to protect this area from flooding.				

Examination question	Name of Case Study	Location	Describe	Explain
▼ *Water landforms and people: Higher Tier*				
Name a water management scheme in an MEDC. (i) Describe the scheme, with the aid of sketches or maps. (ii) Explain how it has affected the lives of people and the environment.				
(i) Name and locate a landform that has been formed or changed by the sea or rivers. (ii) Describe how it was formed, with the aid of sketches or diagrams. (iii) Explain how this landform has affected the lives of people.				
(i) Name and locate a river or coastal landform that has been formed by the sea or rivers. (ii) Describe the landform. (iii) Explain how it is being managed by people.				
(i) Name a place that has been affected by a water shortage. (ii) Describe how the water shortage affected people and places. (iii) Explain what caused the water shortage.				
(i) Name an area where flooding has taken place. (ii) Describe how the flood affected people. (iii) Explain what is being done or what could be done to protect this area from flooding.				

Writing frame for a letter to the Sanjay Gandhi Nagar Residents' Association

Dear Residents' Association

Please find below an explanation of my plan for the development of Sanjay Gandhi Nagar.

The main elements of my plan are................

I have developed the settlement in this way because, for a low cost, I have improved both quality of life and work opportunities. Quality of life has been improved by................

New work opportunities have been created by................

Although my plan has a number of disadvantages including................ I feel that it offers workable solutions that are appropriate to the problems experienced in this LEDC squatter settlement.

I also considered .... and .... but rejected these as being unsuitable because................

Overall, I feel that my plan meets the needs of your community in that................

Yours sincerely

Your name

Answers to terms and meanings

Climate, the environment and people

1	T	7	M	13	S	19	N
2	F	8	I	14	P	20	G
3	O	9	L	15	R	21	U
4	D	10	H	16	K		
5	Q	11	A	17	C		
6	B	12	J	18	E		

Water, landforms and people

1	N	7	K	13	G	19	H
2	R°	8	C	14	M	20	O
3	A	9	Q	15	B	21	T
4	E	10	F	16	P		
5	U	11	S	17	L		
6	I	12	J	18	D		

People and place

1	U	7	S	13	W	19	I
2	N	8	F	14	D	20	G
3	B	9	L	15	J	21	O
4	Q	10	A	16	P	22	M
5	K	11	V	17	E	23	C
6	T	12	H	18	R		

People, work and development

1	V	7	B	13	G	19	I
2	H	8	N	14	L	20	A
3	O	9	E	15	T	21	P
4	D	10	C	16	J	22	K
5	M	11	Q	17	R		
6	U	12	S	18	F		

Answers to questions

Answers to exam practice question on p.19

(a) There is only 1 mark available for this answer so it needs be a relatively simple statement.

The wind blows in a north-westerly direction out of Australia. When it crosses the Equator the direction changes to north-easterly and blows towards India and south Asia.

(1 mark)

(b) You must, in answering this question, make a comparative statement. If you use the word 'whereas' you are almost guaranteed to do this.

The general movement of air in January is the opposite of that in July (1). In January the wind blows in a southerly direction from Asia to Australia (1) whereas in July the direction is northerly from Australia to India (1).

(2 marks)

(c) You have been asked, in this question, to 'explain' so you must give reasons. The question does not, though, say how many reasons to give. This means that you can use either four simple or two elaborated (So what?) statements. An answer similar to the one below would be more than enough to gain all 4 marks:

The movement of air depends on differences in air pressure (1). Air flows from areas of high to low air pressure (1). In June, Australia is relatively cold and so has high air pressure (1) whereas Asia is hot and has low air pressure (1). The wind, therefore, blows from Australia to Asia (1). In July the opposite happens (1).

(4 marks)

(d) Again there are 4 marks being offered and the examiner has put no restrictions on how you gain them. You may, therefore, give four simple or two elaborated (So what?) statements. Make sure that any effects are related to the climate and to the photographs.

Heavy rainfall causes flooding (1) that disrupts transport (1).

The rainfall provides employment opportunities (1) as demand for such items as umbrellas increases (1).

The rain causes flooding of fields (1) providing ideal conditions for the planting of some food crops (1).

(4 marks)

Answers to exam practice question on p.33

(a) Peak rainfall was on 16 July 1997.   **(1 mark)**

(b) The delay between peak rainfall and peak discharge was six days (the difference between peak discharge on 22 July and peak rainfall on 16 July).   **(1 mark)**

(c) In describing the pattern on any line graph you will need to mention the rise and fall of the line, and the rate at which this happens, and quote figures and dates from the axes. In this case you would attract the 3 marks by a statement similar to the following:

The discharge dropped rapidly to 14 July when it reached a low of 1 300 cubic metres per second (cumecs). It then rose equally rapidly to a peak of 3 600 cumecs on 22 July. After that it fluctuated between 3 000 and 3 500 cumecs.

                                    (3 marks)

(d) The 4 marks will be split equally between the two reasons you are asked to give. It is, therefore, a question that asks you to give two elaborated (So what?) answers.
You will gain marks for demonstrating that you understand that the means by which water flows into the rivers after rain has hit the ground takes time and creates the delay. Valid and full answers would be similar to:

Water infiltrates the soil/rocks (1) and travels by through flow/ground water flow slowly to the river (1).

Rain falls on gently sloping land (1) and runs off slowly to the river (1).

There are many trees in the catchment area to intercept the rain (1) so slowing down run-off rates and increasing evapotranspiration (1).

                                    (4 marks)

Answers to exam practice question on p.56

(a) You are asked only to describe what you see in the photograph. Don't be tempted to explain why the housing is there or how it affects the lives of people. Also beware of making value judgements; you may feel that the housing is 'awful' but that is not a description of what you see. Acceptable answers would include:

The houses are small (1), single storey (1), crammed together/have a high density (1). The houses are made of scrap materials (1) or you could make specific reference to the building materials: The house roofs are made of plastic held in place by old tyres (1).

                                    (3 marks)

(b) This question asks you to compare the housing you have just described with that behind it. Make sure that you clearly identify the housing type you are referring to and clearly describe the differences between the two housing types:

These houses have several storeys and are lower than those in the foreground (1).

These houses have been professionally built using concrete unlike those in the foreground that were built by their owners from scrap materials (1).

These high-rise houses have an even higher density than those in the foreground (1).

Individual dwellings in these blocks appear to be larger than those in the foreground (1).

(4 marks)

(c) There are no marks in this question for naming one of the housing types. If you can justify it, the marks are available for explaining how either of the housing types offers the opportunities for a high quality of life.

If you chose the houses in the foreground you may refer to such ideas as:

Large numbers of people living in difficult conditions will pull together (1) creating a positive spirit (1).

As the people have built their own homes (1) they do not have to worry about paying rent (1).

It is much more likely, though, that you have chosen the housing in the background:

Houses are much better built than those in the foreground (1), creating a safer living environment (1).

It is likely that they will have proper sewerage and a tap-water supply unlike those in the foreground (1), encouraging improved health (1).

(4 marks)

Answers to exam practice question on p.73

The answer to this question is different from that for those in the other units. This time, you have chosen the content of your answer. You may have used the information on India from this revision guide or you may have chosen an example from your geography course. So what follows is an explanation as to how you can pick up the highest marks whatever appropriate Case Study you have chosen.

(i) **Name a country or region:** Be careful. You are not asked to name a town or an individual factory. Choose your example carefully. On the other hand, there are no other restrictions, so you may choose an LEDC or MEDC example.
Make sure that you *do* name a country or region.

(ii) **Describe how the job opportunities have changed:** You are being asked to look at a situation in which either jobs have been lost by the closure of an industry, or new jobs have been created by new industry being opened. In this question you are not asked to explain anything but to simply say what has happened. Use as much detail as you have available. Refer to the numbers of jobs lost or created both directly and indirectly. Describe the types of jobs, their skill levels and the different groups of people affected, e.g. school leavers, male/female.

(iii) **Explain how these changes have affected people and the environment:** Now you are being given your chance to explain. You should not have used the word 'because' before now! Note that you are being asked explain how two things have been affected: both people and environments. If you are entered for the Foundation Tier you would expect only to look at *one* of these.

Do you remember the idea of elaborated (So what?) statements? Use them here.

You are being given marks for the quality of your answer and not just for how many simple points you make.

Effects on people of the closure of an industry, for example, may be to create family pressures because of the reduction of money coming into the home. It could create out-migration as people move to other countries or regions in search of employment. It could create greater unemployment for people in service industries as there is less money to spend on leisure, or as the numbers of children fall as a result of out-migration the fewer teachers will be required.

Effects on the environment of the closure of an industry may include dereliction as factory buildings are left empty, and the closure and boarding up of shops and other services as they close down due to lack of custom. There is likely to be a breakdown of the infrastructure as fewer taxes are paid and less public money is available for investment. With large amounts of unemployment there may well be an increase in crime and vandalism, further reducing environmental quality.

In your explanation you must refer to specific examples rather than the vague statements given here. Refer to particular groups of people and specific places and the effects on them.

Have you recognised that what is being described and explained above is the effect of the negative multiplier? Look at it again on page 65 of this revision guide. If you have answered this question by using a situation in which new jobs have been created, you should be able to check out how effective your answer has been by looking at the positive multiplier on page 67.

Finally, the number of marks available for a Case Study question is different according to whether you are entered for the Higher or Foundation Tier. On the Higher Tier it is worth 8 marks compared with only 5 marks on the Foundation Tier. This has implications as to how long you should spend on a Case Study answer. You should spend no more than five minutes on a Foundation Tier answer while for one on the Higher Tier you may allow eight minutes.

Colour resources

▲ **A** Travel problems in Mumbai after flooding during the wet season

▲ **B** Men find work fishing in India, a land that is either flooded or parched

▲ **C** Many people were made temporarily homeless in the Oder floods in Germany, 1997

▲ **D** Transport routes were disrupted after flooding of the Oder

E ▶ Many animals drowned in the Oder

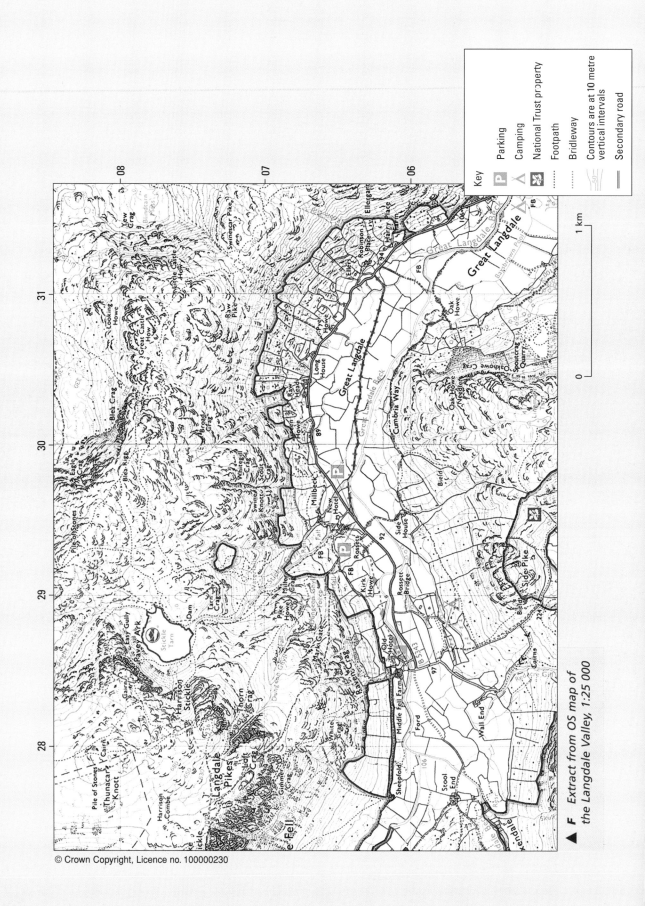

▲ **F** *Extract from OS map of the Langdale Valley, 1:25 000*

Key

P — Parking

△ — Camping

🌳 — National Trust property

⋯⋯ — Footpath

······ — Bridleway

─50─ — Contours are at 10 metre vertical intervals

─── — Secondary road

▲ **G** *Aerial photograph of the Langdale Valley*

▲ **H** *Footpath in Stickle Ghyll,*
Lake District National Park, 1998

1969:	footpath erosion recognised as a problem
1972:	LDNP wardens shovel scree to form a footpath
1973:	volunteers use experimental techniques to construct a footpath to the west of the Ghyll
Late 1970s:	path built as far as the plateau
Early 1980s:	attempts to make a cobbled path
1982:	full-time workers from the Manpower Services Commission's Community Enterprise Scheme take over the work
1983:	bridge built across the Ghyll using a donation from the 'Friends of the Lake District'
1985:	airlift of 700 tonnes of soil and stone to establish vegetation on bare scree
1987:	cobbled path reaches the higher waterfalls

▲ *I   History of footpath protection*
below Stickle Tarn

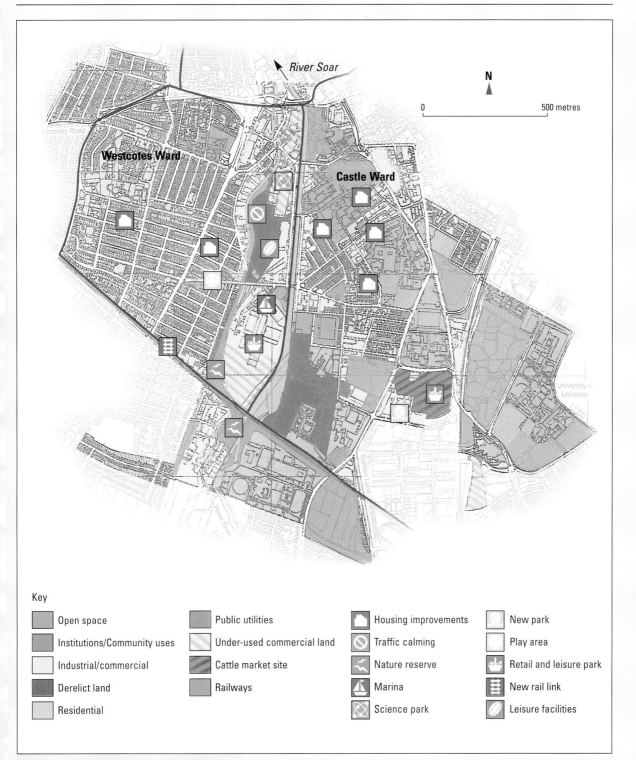

Key

Open space	Public utilities	Housing improvements	New park
Institutions/Community uses	Under-used commercial land	Traffic calming	Play area
Industrial/commercial	Cattle market site	Nature reserve	Retail and leisure park
Derelict land	Railways	Marina	New rail link
Residential		Science park	Leisure facilities

▲ *J Map of the City Challenge Five Year Plan, Leicester, 1993–98*

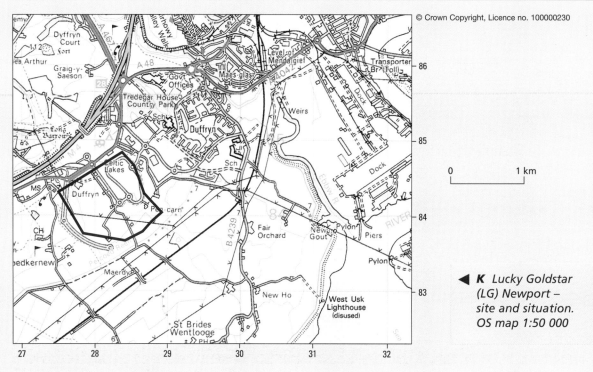

K *Lucky Goldstar (LG) Newport – site and situation. OS map 1:50 000*

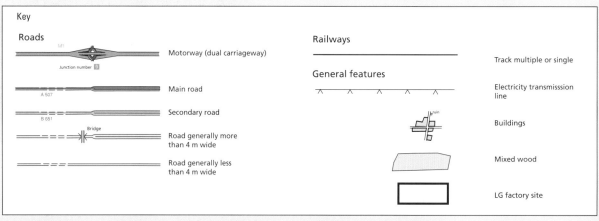

Key

Roads

Motorway (dual carriageway)

Junction number

Main road

Secondary road

Bridge

Road generally more than 4 m wide

Road generally less than 4 m wide

Railways

Track multiple or single

General features

Electricity transmisssion line

Buildings

Mixed wood

LG factory site

L *Site of Lucky Goldstar in Newport, Wales*

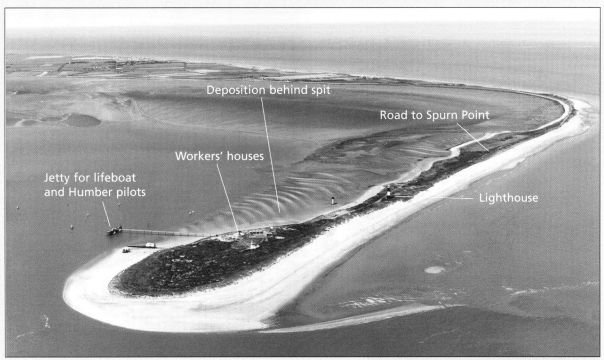

Deposition behind spit

Road to Spurn Point

Workers' houses

Jetty for lifeboat
and Humber pilots

Lighthouse

▲ *M* *Spurn Point on the Holderness coast*

Welds metals

Cost £2,500

Driven by engine
made in India

Runs on diesel

Processes rice
and millet

Generates electricity

▲ *N* *The Village Platform, an electricity generator in Balanfina, Mali*

◀ *O Industrial dereliction in the Ruhr district, Germany*

◀ *P Environment renewal, Emscher Landscape Park, Germany*

Index

Space for your notes